Stranded

Stranded

FINDING NATURE IN UNCERTAIN TIMES

MADDALENA BEARZI

with illustrations by the author

Foreword by
CARL SAFINA

HEYDAY, BERKELEY, CALIFORNIA

Library of Congress Cataloging-in-Publication Data

Names: Bearzi, Maddalena, author, illustrator. | Safina, Carl, 1955- writer
    of foreword.
Title: Stranded: finding nature in uncertain times / Maddalena Bearzi,
    with illustrations by the author; foreword by Carl Safina.
Description: Berkeley, California: Heyday, [2023]
Identifiers: LCCN 2022036214 (print) | LCCN 2022036215 (ebook) |
    ISBN 9781597146043 (hardcover) | ISBN 9781597146135 (epub)
Subjects: LCSH: Natural history—California—Los Angeles. | Nature
    observation—California—Los Angeles. | Urban ecology (Biology)—
    California—Los Angeles. | Los Angeles (Calif.)—Environmental condi-
    tions. | Bearzi, Maddalena. | Women marine biologists—United States—
    Biography.
Classification: LCC QH105.C2 B44 2023 (print) | LCC QH105.C2
    (ebook) | DDC 508.794/94—dc23/eng/20221128
LC record available at https://lccn.loc.gov/2022036214
LC ebook record available at https://lccn.loc.gov/2022036215

Cover Art: Background © 2019 Daboost/Shutterstock;
    Wasp © 2012 irin-k/Shutterstock
Cover Design: Archie Ferguson Design
Cover inset and all interior illustrations: Maddalena Bearzi
Interior Design/Typesetting: Archie Ferguson Design

Published by Heyday
P.O. Box 9145, Berkeley, California 94709
(510) 549-3564
heydaybooks.com

Printed in East Peoria by Versa Press, Inc.

10 9 8 7 6 5 4 3 2 1

FSC
www.fsc.org
MIX
Paper from
responsible sources
FSC® C005010

To Charlie, my lifemate and anchor on Earth

There is pleasure in the pathless woods,
there is rapture on the lonely shore,
there is society where none intrudes, by the deep sea, and music in its roar;
I love not Man the less, but Nature more.

—LORD BYRON

CONTENTS

FOREWORD
Carl Safina

Did you have some kind of life-changing experience during Covid, either big or small?

Of course you did. Me too. We all did.

So it is ironic that this thing that "socially distanced" all of us from each other, from the activities and places that we loved, from things that made us who we thought we were, *also* brings us together now, to tell the stories of how we coped, how we changed, how we adapted as the world swirled around us, how we stopped going far and started going deeper.

Covid was awful.

Covid had a silver lining.

Both things are true.

This book is about some silver linings amid the grief, the shock, the loss.

It was bad. But it wasn't *all* bad. Once we shook off the

shock of going nowhere, many of us blinked and took a new look around. As if for the first time, there they were: our homes, our backyards, our gardens, our pets, the birds, all the creatures who knew nothing of Covid, who do not care about the stock market or what doctors and politicians say. For once, the world stopped getting noisier, our lives stopped getting more frenetic. We had time to think. We had time to *not* think. We could watch. We could remember. We could forget. We could close our eyes and listen.

"The birds are a lot louder this year," said one friend early in the pandemic, before he realized that it wasn't that the birds were any louder; it was that for once in his life he could, finally, hear them.

Author Maddalena Bearzi has lived a life much freer than most, working on the open Pacific Ocean and deriving her bread and butter from following and observing some of the freest creatures in the world—wild dolphins. So when the pandemic came, the cessation of everything, and a new life confined to virtual house arrest, came as a shock to her way of being. We can all relate.

But even if life seemed to give up on us, Maddalena wasn't going to give up on life, on living. So she pivoted. Turning her curiosity and her powers of observation onto her home, her yard, the quotidian creatures who come and go—including some she'd never before noticed—Maddalena did what most of us had to do. She rode out the grief, recalibrated, paid attention to great gifts in little packages, and came to understand that the little things are also the big things. And fortunately for us, she wrote about it all and has given it to us in the compulsively readable pages that follow.

So, pour something for yourself. Get comfortable. You're in for a treat. Now turn the page.

I

FOLLOWING FLUKEPRINTS

It's approaching 3:00 p.m. The water is unruffled and a thick coat of fog has devoured the City of Angels. We have been at sea for several hours, and now, four miles offshore from the California coast, there is no trace of shore, birds, whales, or dolphins. No sky or horizon, no point of reference.

Charlie cuts the haze with the bow of the boat, keeping an eye on the radar and munching pretzels. My research team and I, damp and weary but still attentive, scan what little is discernible through the dense blanket of mist. The laptop computer is on, set to collect data at five-minute intervals as dictated by my protocol, binoculars and cameras are out, hydrophones and plankton net are on deck, ready for deployment.

We are silent, floating off the coastline above one of those ocean "freeways" called fronts, where merging distinct masses of water create a current or temperature differential in which a diversity of marine life tends to congregate. Against the soothing backdrop of this almost surreal SoCal day, I look down into the unknown, dark liquid world so dissimilar from my own.

• • •

Standing on the cobblestones outside the trattoria *Papaveri e Papere*, in Milan, Northern Italy, now many years ago, Charlie and I had instantly become friends; shortly after that, lovers. He has always been bright, charming, industrious, and endowed with uncanny humor and robust common sense. From the beginning, we talked almost every night, our conversations extended into the late hours, sometimes lasting through dawn's first light.

On one of those cold *Milanese* evenings, he shared difficult news. "I will have to go back to Los Angeles soon," he said with a mournful tone in his California accent. But then, as a shiver started running down my spine, he asked, "Would you move there with me?"

I was twenty-nine, and in the blink of an eye I let out a resounding *yes!* And I hugged him.

Luggage packed and the Italian chapter of my life

sealed, I headed ten thousand miles away from my country with a bachelor's degree in natural science, a job as a photo-journalist, an ongoing position as principal investigator for a sea turtle study in the Celestún Reserve of Yucatán, a *prosciutto* thigh, two bottles of *Amarone*, and a fresh set of dreams.

We settled into a small apartment overlooking the docks of Marina del Rey harbor, where I often watched the wondrous scarlet sky dimming into a pitch-black night. I couldn't have been happier.

Scalawag was a forty-foot racing sailboat Charlie had kept from his regatta days, which now floated in her slip about a block from our flat. She was worn down by time and neglect and in serious need of a makeover. We rolled up our sleeves, and in the course of a month or two, brought her back to life.

Aboard *Scalawag*, we sailed off Los Angeles every week-end. We were both drawn to the water like bears to beehives, for different reasons. For me, the Pacific ocean meant quietude and boundless nature to explore. For Charlie, it was the much-needed respite from his frantic job. My husband-to-be was more comfortable at sea than in any terrestrial place, as if he had saltwater in his veins. And because he understood and respected the ocean, Charlie had the soul and skill of an old sea captain. In his expert hands, I would have sailed to the moon.

The ocean became our second home. Pounding into a

shattering Santa Ana breeze, lulled by gentle swells, rocked by a short chop, sun-blasted or fogged in, we were there, blowing in the California wind, Charlie standing at the helm, relentlessly attentive, sailing as fast as possible, as though he was dashing against a team of invisible racing boats. The farther and the choppier, the better it was for him. I would sit either caressing the waves with my feet, or up against the mast, hands clutching the shrouds, gazing ever-seaward, binoculars around my neck.

I have never been good at idle. At sea or on land, I am a nosey bee, always probing my environment. Now, there it was, the Southern California Bight, to me, a new territory to be uncovered. I didn't know what yet, but unquestionably, offshore of this sprawling city and the raucous traffic of the Pacific Coast Highway, something worth noticing awaited.

It was during those first several months of weekend-only outings that I became aware of the remarkable presence of dolphin, whale, and pinniped (seal and sea lion) species off Los Angeles.

Before setting foot in LA, I'd studied the behavior of many marine mammal species in far-flung locations. Yet, I had never experienced such diversity in one place; and here it was, at my fingertips.

Back on land, with memory as the only register of all I was seeing off the city's shores, I dug into the scientific literature for information on the local cetaceans (whales, dolphins, and porpoises), sure to unearth oodles. But to my disbelief, I found next to nothing. Offshore from a metropolis of nearly ten million human souls, nobody had ever studied these animals, even if some traveled just feet away from the crowded beaches. They were strangers among us.

For me, the Bight was a place of mystery teeming with life. I felt awe and joy, all at once.

Back aboard *Scalawag* and armed with patience, pencil, paper, and the power of observation, I started recording opportunistic data on my new marine friends and their day-in-day-out activities, habits, and quirks. I had no plans. No hypotheses to speak of. The water was a waiting canvas to be colored by the antics of whatever wild species were out there.

That marked a new chapter in my everyday life spent in the company of California dolphins and whales as well as the beginning of what has become one of the longest-running marine mammal studies, not only along the West Coast of the United States but worldwide.

As time unfurled and my understanding of this unique patch of ocean grew, my preliminary handwritten logs—largely based on my prior cetacean investigations in the Gulf of Mexico, Caribbean, and Mediterranean seas—evolved into an all-inclusive, complex dataset of my own design entered into a laptop computer: a comprehensive collection of information on oceanographic conditions and an array of organisms encountered, from humpbacks to sunfish.

My penciled notes on methodology grew into a technical research protocol as thick as the Bible. Our two-member crew became a team of trained assistants and volunteers. From binoculars and a notepad, the research equipment now lived in a stack of Pelican cases filled with multiple still cameras, video cameras, underwater hydrophones, radio headsets, laptop computers, plankton nets, GPS devices, and more. And my observations spawned multiple and new hypotheses. Even the restored *Scalawag*, with Charlie's blessing, was traded for a more suitable offshore research boat. Charlie and I then together envisioned and cofounded the Ocean Conservation Society. Our mission: conduct long-term marine mammal research and educational projects for the protection of the ocean and marine wildlife. A calling we have been fully committed to for more than twenty-five years.

• • •

Forty-five minutes after arriving in the Bight this afternoon, many years into my research to better understand the lives of dolphins and whales, I am still waiting. Waiting for a sudden movement on the surface, a dark fin emerging from the depths, a blow exploding mist into this already misty air.

Around 4:00 p.m., twelve pelicans with their massive bills pass by in tidy procession like miniature monks heading to their cells. As they swiftly disappear into the fog, the brown heads of a California sea lion duo break the surface.

"One sea lion leaping . . . starboard side!" Charlie shouts, pointing to another individual rocketing out of the water just next to the hull. The pinniped slows down, glances at us, and waves one pectoral fin in the air in a sort of "Hey!" interspecies greeting.

The sea lion threesome now dashes ahead in unison, and with no dolphins in sight, we shadow this cluster of pinniped torpedoes through banks of foggy impenetrability. Three individuals become five, and out of nowhere, five become twenty, all ducking in and out of the wavelets toward deeper waters. A few times, they slow down, spyhopping like submarine periscopes in search of enemy ships. Then, fine-tuning their direction and in full porpoising mode, they dart into a new fog bank. We speed up to follow.

As streaks of sunlight begin to pierce the fog barricade, an unexpected scene opens in front of us. The sea lions have infiltrated an area occupied by fifty-plus common dolphins. Glossy, with long, slender beaks and an hourglass pattern on each side, the dolphins rise and vanish headfirst into what seems a massive pot of boiling water. In a feeding frenzy, the dolphins spin and dive into swirling balls of anchovies, loosing

7

an inverse rainstorm of glittering scales that rise to the surface. The less agile pinnipeds are orbiting the dolphins, emulating these cetaceans by swiveling and dipping down in attempts to seize their own share of fish. In the air, flocks of squawking and sharp-eyed California seagulls and elegant terns hover, eager to plunge and claim the leftovers. A few pelicans with fish-filled gular pouches float on the surface lulled by wavelets. The anchovies swarm in even tighter baitballs in a last-ditch defensive measure against the array of predators attacking from every direction. Off to the side and maintaining a distance, us. Boat at idle, we listen to this fluid symphony of clicks and whistles and squeals, and watch this marvelous act occurring at the boundary of sea and sky. There is no aggression or hostility; food is plentiful for everyone to share.

Abruptly, as if Moses had willed it, the swirling mass in the water parts. The boiling pot is now divided into two small gyres and in the middle, the eerie, slender figure of a ten-foot blue shark takes shape. The tip of its dorsal fin gently touches the air before this top predator plummets to penetrate one of the lingering whirling fish balls that grow smaller by the minute. Sea lions and birds are now mere bystanders, spectators of something larger and more powerful. On the edges of the gyres, handfuls of common dolphins resume eating, lunging upside down to snatch the last remaining anchovies.

The fog has raised its veil, and the feast has come to an end with nothing remaining but shimmering streams of diamond-like scales. The shark is gone. In rank formation, the dolphins leap northward at speed, and all we can see are splashes and flukes then more splashes in the distance, until the splashes are gone and the water resumes its lake-like veneer. The sea lions have dispersed in random directions. We head west toward port and home; behind us, an orange sun bathes the horizon. We are soundless, still enchanted by the almost spiritual beauty of this *mise-en-scène* only the ocean can offer.

• • •

It took that chilly, hazy day, chasing sea lions in pursuit of dolphins searching for prey, to spark my curiosity about interspecies encounters—encounters that seemed not spontaneous to me. My job as a behavioral ecologist implies the study of how and why behaviors vary to "fit" the environment that human and nonhuman animals live in, and by doing so help us better understand the variety of ways creatures eat, avoid predation, mate, and rear their offspring. Here, I had the sense pinnipeds were cleverly taking advantage of the dolphins' knack for echolocating food. Cetaceans are equipped with something impressive that pinnipeds don't have. Thanks to their mighty biological sonar, dolphins are masters of *seeing* with sound, pinpointing prey at great distance. I started following sea lions seeking dolphins, and recording their aggregations.

Only later, after plodding through and analyzing seemingly endless hours of videotape that made one seasick to watch for the bobbing up and down of the camera, was I able to corroborate my hypothesis. Sea lions do, indeed, look for common dolphins to exploit these cetaceans' superior ability to echolocate prey in the open ocean, where resources are patchy.

That's how my brain works at sea. It starts with three simple and inexpensive ingredients: curiosity about nature *en bloc*, observation or the power of seeing or taking notice of something, and perhaps most importantly, an open mind. Practicing observation is a little like staying ultra-still for hours during a mediation session. It obliges time and patience. It's through paying attention to the whole that questions arise in my mind. These are hypotheses, nothing more than ideas and assumptions suggested for the sake of argument for things I believe may be true.

The next essential ingredient is literature research. It's definitely less exciting than being among dolphins because it demands hours sitting in front of a computer screen, glasses on, digging deep into what's known about the topic at hand, if anything. But this determines whether an idea is worth pursuing or needs further tweaking. A simple hypothesis can mushroom into others, all in need of answers that entail experimentation and, later on, the quantifying and analyzing of often massive data sets. Answers usually breed more questions in the unremitting cycle of science.

• • •

Over many years, led by curiosity and dedication, my research team and I have had countless encounters with the wild and mysterious marine mammals off the teeming City of Angels.

We saw Pacific white-sided dolphins close off Malibu, showing off the natural beauty of their two-tone physiques in astounding midair somersaults. With a languid mood, bottlenose dolphins traveled and foraged up and down the coast in almost perpetual motion. They were constantly changing group composition in their fluid fission-fusion societies, much like people shifting from one social cluster to another at a party. On occasion, transient, mammal-eating orcas, with their monochrome black fins and cultural traditions passed from generation to generation, roamed in pursuit of a meal: a baby gray whale, a sea lion, an occasional seabird. Pacific harbor seals slept on sun-kissed rocks or relaxed in kelp beds just shouting distance from Hollywood celebrities' garish and well-guarded mansions. Offshore, shadowy Dall's porpoises dashed with gravity-defying leaps, their dorsal fins carving through the surface with such swiftness a watery "rooster tail" was all one could see. Standoffish and bulky Risso's dolphins, oddly dissimilar in temper from the affable ones I met in the Tyrrhenian Sea, made brief appearances before fading into the depths in search of squiddy buffets. We tailed gargantuan blue whales, with blowholes so big a baby could fit inside them, and humpback whales, with their endlessly evolving, haunting and beautiful songs. I learned as much as I could about their otherworldly complex and magical existence, especially that of the whales and dolphins, who captivated me the most. And I started to understand how much they share with us, the striking resemblances, and the linkages among different species and their collective habitat—those invisible ties that exist in the intertwining webs of marine life. I saw firsthand how every living organism at sea plays a part; how every being is essential for the survival of others in a delicate balance.

• • •

Life in LA revolved around the work Charlie and I do for and with the ocean. Then all of a sudden, on a seemingly ordinary morning at the outset of spring, that life vanished.

The flowers in my garden were blooming; the sky was its usual intense California blue; the dog next door was barking with his high-pitched voice. On my desk lay the airplane ticket for Europe, where it had been sitting for over a week.

My iPhone squawked, showing another incoming text from my mom: "Don't come!!! It's a mess here!!!!!" I remember scrolling down to read the rest of my mother's exclamation point-filled dispatch reaching me from the other side of the planet, sadly learning how Italy was already strangled in the grip of the Coronavirus.

That day changed everything for me. And for everyone else on Earth.

With no other choice on the horizon, we did what other nonhuman animals on Earth do: we adapted. We stayed home, we avoided crowds, we wore masks and reduced activities to the purely essential. And then there was the awkwardness of social distancing and Zoom meetups, swapping our natural contact with others for sterile face-to-face conversations on computer screens. It was a new domain, an unfamiliar creek to navigate with no paddles or easy instructions. Confusion, panic, and fear were everywhere.

As a field marine biologist accustomed to spending most of the time outside and in the wild, I found this new regime stifling. For so many scientists whose jobs depend on being out in the world searching to further understand nature beyond human borders, our lives' purpose was upended. You can't work from home when your work *is* the ocean. Not that I had any right to complain. I was living in my house with a loving husband, a dog, a backyard, and everything I needed, toilet paper included. But I still couldn't circumvent the caged feeling of being closed inside four walls.

With my research shuttered because of the unforeseen, meteor-like impact of a pandemic, unable to be at sea with my team due to social distancing, I could only revisit in my mind that vivid day when the anchovies arrived, that simple act of feeding, interacting, living. I was sequestered, stopped in my tracks and blocked from being on the water, where I have spent much of my life. I yearned for the ocean and that lost, almost spiritual connection with the dolphins.

2

A CITY DWELLER IN DISGUISE

It has been months since I have been able to venture out on the ocean to study the dolphins. I think about the individual bottlenose I have met and photo-identified off the LA shores over the many years. Sadmom, Mozza, Halfmoon, Scarface, Bump, Allnotch, Gnocco, Eos, Gandalf, and many others. People say you don't really miss something until it's gone, and the dolphins are gone to me now. I see them only in my memories and dreams.

Shut inside the house, I feel something has vanished from my life, something vital to who I am.

I don't believe I am grief-stricken. Uncertain periods are a part of living; things change, sometimes quickly, sometimes for the worse. As a pragmatist, I also realize the virus hasn't dramatically altered my existence or that of my loved ones as it has for many other people on Earth. I am privileged. Yet, I am a witness to the sorrow hovering around me and elsewhere in the world.

While I've always been good at pulling myself up by my bootstraps and finding a way out from the occasional kick of despair, this particular afternoon, deprived of human and nonhuman friends, there is a veil of sadness that envelops me, and it doesn't want to let go.

To sweep off this seemingly inescapable sense of melancholy, I decide to keep my brain engaged by undertaking a spring cleaning of my garage. While digging into timeworn boxes, I come across a fading black-and-white photo of a tiny version of myself in my mom's arms. In the image, I wore a pale sweater knitted by Grandma, and I held a stuffed yellow dog with floppy ears, beaded eyes, and stained fur. It was the first animal I ever owned, and it felt real to me. It wasn't long after this picture was taken that I started rescuing real animals, beseeching my initially reluctant parents to welcome them into our home and backyard.

• • •

During my childhood, I spent many summers camping out with

my family in Orvile, a pristine and remote site in Sardinia. It was there, in front of a turquoise sea, a lagoon streaked with emerald-green shades and miles of untouched shores, that my love affair with nature began.

In Sardinia, I explored the small creatures of the sand, collected shells of any shape and size, snorkeled in a sea full of life. I ate fresh-caught mussels, lobster, seabass, and octopi. I ran wildly among flocks of sheep and horses in the hills near our campsite. I played war games with my brother Gio using handfuls of dead seagrass leaves of *Posidonia oceanica* as ammunition. And I was happy as a clam.

My parents always let me roam free; they were never obsessed with safety. They figured if I got pinched by a crab or stepped on a sea urchin, next time I would be more careful. And I did, and I was. Learn from your experiences: that was my dad's credo. It brought me so close to nature at an early age.

Sardinia was a paradise, a place to observe, touch, and explore the wild in all corners as though civilization had never existed; a place to fill my lungs with pure, natural air. But that was only in the summertime; for the rest of the year, I lived in the city. So, I opened my own personal window on nature to keep inhaling that almost whimsical scent of my days in Sardinia.

Living far from the sea wasn't going to stop me.

I was initially captivated by large species such as lions, tigers, and elephants, and I became almost obsessed with knowing more about their marvelous worlds. Through the words of writers, I vicariously traveled from Africa to India, from Asia to Madagascar. I filled my dreams with images, fantasizing about being out there, among the great carnivores, working side by side and in the wild with some of the most renowned biologists of the seventies.

But I wasn't there. Not even close. I was an urban girl, living in a town of manicured lawns and neat rows of grungy trees along paved roadways. It was clear to me that wildlife had lost the battle for survival within the walls of my Northern Italian city.

With no imminent hope of traveling alone to the faraway habitats I craved because of my young age, I decided to make do. First, I rescued a cat, and then a dog. Later on, lizards, tortoises, and snakes found in the hills nearby expanded my biota assemblage in my parents' courtyard. With mom's consent, half of the garden was converted into a terrarium where different reptilian species were peacefully cohabiting.

As a child, I loved collecting—and later releasing—any sort of animal; it didn't matter if it was ugly, furry, scaley, slimy, or sheltered in a carapace. I crafted a micro version of wilderness, and all my gathered fauna became the subject of my first naive observations.

Armed with a notebook and pencil, I learned to design simple experiments in "nature." Under the hot sun, on foggy or rainy days, after school or during the weekends, I spent hours transcribing the behavior of the lizards coming in and out the crannies of my dad's brick grill, or the feeding habits of a tortoise rescued from a busy road a few years earlier. I cyclically scrutinized the activities of Yoghi, my rescued German shepherd mix, hoping to discover something yet unknown about his kind.

None of these experiments went very far in terms of prodigious breakthroughs, but they allowed me to see the beauty in any species, and to stay close to nature despite my life as a city dweller.

• • •

I close the box teeming with memories along with the garage door, the storage area now scoured to cleanliness, and walk outside to my backyard. I still feel downhearted.

As I angle my lounge chair on the weathered grass toward the sun, I see a female western fence lizard. She is basking on a slice of bark peeling off the Indian laurel fig tree.

I never even noticed lizards in my garden until this very moment.

She follows a patch of light with teeny movements, soaking up the leftover rays of the sun and spreading her body against the tree trunk to extend her surface area for more rapid absorption of energy. I track her as she explores the northern corner of the yard, seemingly uncaring of my gigantic hominid presence. Her length is just slightly bigger than my pinky.

Splashes of auburn above the eyes fashion drag-queenish makeup on her small head. It's the unique maquillage females of this species often wear in the spring breeding season. Her overall sandy-brown color is paler than that of males, broken by dark, horizontal chevrons; and the sharply keeled scales on her back and sides are easily discernable even from where I sit.

• • •

One time, at a dinner party Charlie and I threw before the term "social distancing" was invented, I was talking to my friend Dan Blumstein, an ethologist and conservation biologist, like me. Tall, skinny, with oval-shaped glasses, and curious by nature, Dan studies the evolution of social behavior and communication of yellow-bellied marmots at the Rocky Mountain Biological Lab in Colorado. And like me, he is an odd scientist, in the sense that every sort of animal—and how it responds to human-induced habitat changes—captures his interest.

Between forkfuls of *rigatoni all'amatriciana* and gulps of *Chianti*, we chatted about my fieldwork on the lizards of a nat-ural reserve in Tuscany back in my early days as a student, and he told me about a recent investigation he and his colleagues conducted on western fence lizards.

"We discovered that these western populations have significant differences in morphological characters associated with urban sprawl and temperature across four dissimilar sites in Southern California," Dan explained to me while cleaning the last bit of sauce from his plate with a slice of baguette.

"What we noticed," he continued, "is that in more developed areas like LA, the length of the limbs and hind toes decrease. City lizards are more robust with shorter and stouter limbs than their outdoorsy counterparts living in natural woody substrates. And this, of course, is consistent with the characteristics of their microenvironment and how they use it. . . . Ultimately, having short legs and toes works better in urban settings!"

As Charlie served him a second plate of pasta, Dan resumed, "Urban lizards have fewer dorsal scales too. This change in morphology helps them to lessen evaporative water loss by diminishing the surface area of living skin cells between the scales. Reduced vegetation and increased hardscape, you know, can make urban areas warmer than natural areas, creating the so-called *urban heat island effect*, so minimizing water loss is important for these small critters."

"Isn't that cool?"

Recalling that conversation, I focus in even more on my backyard western fence lizard. I don't have a countryside lizard to compare her with; this one, though, is definitely a robust specimen with short, stout limbs. Unquestionably *cool*!

Despite observing animals most of my life it still astounds me how, in many places, they must constantly, and at times rapidly, evolve to adapt to our incessant habitat destruction.

• • •

My western fence is on the go, probably probing for ants or spiders. Following this little reptile is inarguably unlike tailing wide-ranging whales and dolphins on the open ocean. My head doesn't even need to move to make out her actions; they all occur right in front of my eyes. Yet, there is something engaging and joyful about narrowing my field of observation on this tiny creature and her behavior, all effortlessly served up in my backyard.

Suddenly, I see myself as a young girl, back in the microscopic version of wildlife of my parents' *giardino*, watching the lizards coming in and out the cracks of Dad's brick barbeque. It was those first raw observations that, a few decades ago, drew me close to Mother Nature when there was no other place for me to go.

As my scientific mind rambles on with questions about

western fence lizards, I notice that the feelings of despair have begun to dissipate. And with them, my newly discovered, pocket-size acquaintance has now vanished into the lush foliage of a fig vine on the backyard wall.

So there I am. Decades later, on the other side of the planet, with a Ph.D. in biology, a postdoc, and more than thirty years of field experience under my belt, I find myself observing lizards and other landbound wild animals visiting the garden of my rented home in Los Angeles, just as I did in my youth back in Italy.

I see squirrels teasing my dog Genghis from the branches of the Chinese strawberry tree in an incessant conflict with no losers or winners. While drinking morning coffee, I follow the astonishing wingbeats of tiny Anna's, Rufous, and Allen's hummingbirds sucking a few drops of nectar out of a flower every few seconds. At night, I wait for my mutt to smell the neighborhood skunk; then, we snoop it out together through the window, careful to avoid being sprayed by its notorious defensive weapon scent. Sometimes, a raccoon or an opossum comes by to eat my plants and fallen fruits, providing me with yet another opportunity to watch their meticulous ways of foraging.

When I finally opened my eyes, I rediscovered that there is so much wilderness to observe around me, even without leaving home. And once again, I feel that same bursting curiosity toward these urban-dwelling creatures that I did as a child.

3

COYOTE KNOCKING AT MY DOOR

They say coyotes are at the door but I must have been out because I missed them today. Here in our suburban neighborhood, they say coyotes are walking in packs among us. They say they are going to eat our children playing in the backyard and take away our freedom to be outside. They say we must shoot them if they cross our path. They say we should build a Trumpian wall between us and them to protect ourselves. *They* have a place to say all these things: it's called Nextdoor.

Nextdoor is the online "local hub to connect and share with the neighborhood. The place where communities come together to keep a local shopkeeper in business. Where neighbors exchange recommendations for babysitters, plans for local events, and tips about what to order at that new café down the street. Welcome to Nextdoor!"

What Nextdoor doesn't mention in its friendly "connect with our neighborhoods" advertising is that, at times, it is also the place where community connection can turn into mob mentality.

As a behavioral ecologist, the latest barrage from some concerned Nextdoorians affected me personally when they went after a local animal I love and respect: the coyote.

• • •

My house sits near the top of a quiet Westside residential knoll of Los Angeles, less than ten minutes by car from the Pacific Ocean. Down the hill, the once pristine wetland marsh, rich with endemic species, has been slowly chewed away by the Playa Vista enclave, now known as Silicon Beach. This is an upscale commercial and housing development—with homes that go for more than two million dollars—foolishly placed on top of large, underground pockets of highly flammable methane gas.

Along the still untouched natural bluffs overlooking Playa Vista, with a view of Los Angeles that spans from the ocean to the Hollywood sign, I walk my dog on the dirt trails that leave stretch marks of urban sprawl across the slopes. As we stroll, the mutt and I sniff blossoming spring flowers and green grass, along with sporadic whiffs of methane seeping out of the ground below us.

These bluffs are the closest nature we can experience on foot. Here, a few steps from an army of Google techies, a postage-stamp-sized patch of wildlife endures.

Along the incline, desert cottontails rest under shrub canopies and arboreal eastern fox squirrels collect acorns. There are raccoons, opossums, and skunks preying on mice while red-tailed and Cooper's hawks soar overhead and super-charged hummingbirds sip nectar out of indigenous plants. Lizards thermoregulate on the sizzling Cali rocks and elusive rattlesnakes rest under woodpiles.

Here, a stone's throw from the teeming 405 freeway, coyotes found a home.

• • •

For eons, coyotes roamed the open prairies of the West. Then, as white settler-colonizers pushed in, killing wolves and mountain lions, coyotes spread unhindered into most of North America. On their way to new lands, these canines had to deal with legions of hunters armed with poison, guns, and traps. But the misguided war that settlers waged against wildlife only helped wipe out coyotes' larger and stronger natural competitors, making this West's wild dog even more resilient.

Outlasting human onslaughts, persecutions, and attempts at annihilation, they thrived, disseminating like weeds to every corner of the continent.

Coyotes are true American survivors. When they find themselves under pressure from hunters, their packs split up into pairs or single individuals. They generate larger litters and migrate into new territories. And with wilderness becoming rare due to our obsession with growth that destroys these predators' natural habitat, we now force them to live among us; and they are here to stay.

• • •

I walk my dog every day wondering whether I am going to see one of these unique canines with their thick, rusty gray-blond fur and bushy tails. And what do they see when they look at us and what we've made of their home? Through their keen yellow-mustard eyes, Los Angeles has to be very different from what their ancestors, now buried in the La Brea tar pits, experienced a long time ago.

Coyotes, smaller in size and more svelte than their close relative, the gray wolf, were here long before LA was LA; before downtown skyscrapers, freeways, strip malls, car-filled parking lots, and Playa Vistas. This land belongs to them more than it belongs to us, and coyotes have no intention of leaving because this is where the food is.

These animals are like us in many ways. They are opportunists, fighters, quick learners, and problem solvers. They are complex, clever sentient beings with their own personalities. And as we become more and more of an urban species, coyotes do too.

With an acute sense of smell and the ability to run more than forty miles per hour, these skilled and crafty predators are not picky eaters, feeding on pretty much anything that fits in their mouth, from rodents to insects; even garbage makes it onto their menu.

Urban sprawl has forced coyotes to swap their natural food preferences for a more trash-based diet. It's no surprise these adaptive city dwellers are cozying up to us, feasting on free, easy buffets of leftovers, fruit, and the occasional small domestic pet. I empathize with the fear and pain of those who have lost a beloved four-legged companion to the jaws of a coyote. Yet, we must find ways to cohabitate.

To elude us, coyotes have turned mostly nocturnal, living scrappy, clandestine urban existences, and hiding their dens in the most unexpected corners. But we are doing little to find viable solutions and allow them enough wild habitat to live on. Most of us have no idea about the vital role they play in the ecosystem, helping to keep rodent populations on a tight rein. And we don't realize that these animals are more wary of us than we are of them.

• • •

The Nextdoorians' coyote panic seems to have kicked into an even higher gear in the last few days. In a recent post, some lady espoused the use of Kevlar dog suits to protect her pair of Pomeranians from coyotes trespassing on her lawn. She swears these outfits are good for cats too. In the crescendo of anti-coyote hysteria, building a wall on the top of the bluffs and bearing rifles for defense are popular this week, but not as much as the new *Coyotes: Be Aware!* signs that are popping up like mushrooms in the groomed front yards near my home. Many neighbors loved the idea on the Nextdoor page a few weeks back, adorning the post with thumbs-up and smiling emojis. Now, *Coyotes: Be Aware!* signs are everywhere. And the coyotes must be reading them with sharp eyes and staying very aware, because I still haven't spotted any today.

As Genghis sniffs and considers peeing on one of the signs in question, I wonder what fuels this human hatred of coyotes. Why are the Nextdoorians panicking at only the innuendo of a coyote? What fosters their desire to dismiss, exclude, and destroy? Is the coyote-phobia powered by ignorance about this species, or is there more? Are we middle-class Americans so used to being safe without even thinking about it that having to live with alertness to threats and take precautions against coyotes is seen as an outrageous demand? Do I feel differently because I have spent most of my existence studying the behavior of wild animals, and they haven't? Why can't they see these canines as I do? As fascinating large street dogs coming out mostly under the protection of darkness. Unkempt perhaps, but clever, versatile, and resilient.

It's likely all of the above. And not knowing coyotes—or not wanting to know them—certainly has much to do with it. We *Homo sapiens* frequently dread what we don't understand. Often, our fears are much scarier than real life. And instead of asking questions, learning more, and developing a curiosity about these four-legged fellows, instead of humbly sharing our neighborhoods with them, we overreact.

But it's only by opening our minds, not leaping to conclusions and fearing nature, that we begin to see and appreciate the wildlife that surrounds us.

• • •

In my search for coyotes trotting around the neighborhood, I put my Sherlock Holmes hat on. It's a different hat from the one I wear to track dolphins and whales at sea, although they both embody learning and perseverance.

Coyote tracks and scats are one way to pinpoint their movements, and if identifying these clues takes a little research, a field guide—or the internet, for that matter—will suffice.

Overall, their footprints are oval-shaped and smaller

than a baby's hand; the paws have four toes with claws, each with a roughly triangular heel pad. At first sight, they might look the same as Genghis's footprints, but dog tracks are rounder and less symmetrical, with blunted nails. Plus, in a coyote's paw, there is a larger negative space between toes and pad than in a dog's. These elusive canines also walk in straight lines, while domestic dogs tend to veer to one side or the other.

Scats are usually grayish, unscented, tubular, and rope-like, with spongy consistency, measuring less than one inch in diameter. Because of the coyote's omnivorous diet, an all-inclusive sampling of fauna and flora can be present therein: berries, nuts, garden crops, grass, leaves, hair, bones from mice and rats, and heaps of other delicious tidbits.

I've seen coyote tracks and scats frequently while walking along the dirt paths of the Playa Vista bluffs, but in the entire time I have lived here, I have rarely spotted them close to home.

Along with following their paw prints and poop, I tried howling, as coyotes are known to howl back. So far, there has been no response to my high-pitched calls. It may be just that my Italian howl is not to their liking.

From my time in the wilderness, I realize nature doesn't play on my terms and patience is of the essence. Lizards, geckos, birds, sea turtles, dolphins, and whales have taught me that during many years in the field. I've learned to wait for all sorts of animals; and the reward was (almost) always worth the wait.

• • •

Genghis has finished sniffing, and our walk in the backwoods of deep suburbia resumes. This early morning, instead of howling or searching for tracks, I decide to use Nextdoor to my own benefit. Phone out of my jeans' pocket, I open the Nextdoor app. Under notifications, and with the title "*Coyote Alert! Corner of Kentwood Avenue and Riggs Place! Be Safe Out There!*," someone just posted a blurry photo of an alleged coyote. Alleged because the image is so out of focus and taken from so far away that the creature in it could easily be a long-legged scruffy pooch that lost its way. It wouldn't be the first time people have mistaken domestic pets for coyotes in our area. But I recognize the street name and it's only a couple of blocks from me. Pulling my dog, who would rather stop every few seconds than participate in the hypothetical coyote quest, I head toward Kentwood Avenue.

Reaching the corner, I howl, I look for tracks and scats, all the while checking Nextdoor to see if there are updates on the sighting. Nothing. No signs of a coyote around here.

I wouldn't be surprised if the next photo posted on Nextdoor's notification page is one of me: "*Crazy Person Alert! Woman howling in the middle of the street with spotted dog. Corner of Kentwood Avenue and Riggs Place! Be Safe Out There!*"

I close the app and mull over the idea of using Nextdoor, like the free platform iNaturalist, as a means to raise awareness instead of fostering fear of the coyotes in our midst. In a perfect world, Nextdoorians could be valuable citizen scientists, taking notes and sharing sightings of this elusive wild creature they currently view as an enemy.

Sitting on the curb, I type several paragraphs under today's *Coyote Alert!* post explaining my perspective and throwing in my ideas of how we might build a new suburban wildlife ethic for living together. Then, I continue my walk, still hoping for a coyote encounter.

Back at home, I can't resist opening the Nextdoor page to check whether anyone has taken the hook. And there it is, a deluge of replies. Most are bleak, bordering on rude; scrolling down, though, I read some positive reactions too. And I see a shred of hope.

Indeed, we—Nextdoorians and humans in general—still have a lot to learn from coyotes. Even with our attempts to put nature in order, far from the neatness of our houses, this versatile overcomer teaches us an essential lesson about coexistence. The coyotes tell us we need to learn respect and compassion, and how to thrive with other nonhuman beings with whom we share this Earth.

· · ·

They say coyotes are at my doorstep but I missed them again today. I always miss them.

At times, I hear the distant howl of a coyote at dusk in one of those rare moments when the city turns down its background volume. I think it's such a gift to listen to this sound, once the symbol of the American West. I think I am fortunate to live near these incredible indigenous, wild animals whose roots go back five million years.

4

MY DOG IS NOT THE SMARTEST COOKIE IN THE JAR

Our dog is a rescued male mix. Half labrador and half great dane, he has a pink belly and a white coat speckled with black spots.

He sits next to us, waiting for the next stroll.

At first, Charlie and I named him Angus, after Angus Young, guitar player for the band AC/DC. That name didn't stick long with our puppy; due to my thick Italian accent, Angus sounded too much like *Anus* when I called him. So, we renamed him Genghis after the great Genghis Khan, thinking he would grow up to be as large as a great dane and as fearless as the Emperor of the Mongol Empire. But he didn't. Our dog is an oversized lab with harlequin dane fur and the face of a mutt; plus, he gets skittish if a fly goes by.

Charlie thinks Genghis is not the smartest cookie in the jar because he normally doesn't respond to commands. As I see it, Genghis is clever *precisely* for the reason that he doesn't obey either one of us well. After more than eight years in our company, I am sure our dog knows what we say to him. He just doesn't care to act upon it, further pushing the envelope of what he can get away with. And I know this because if I say, "What did I tell you?" once or twice, Genghis—reluctantly and with a snort of disapproval—does what he's told.

• • •

Before Genghis came into our life, we did have a very clever dog. He was named Burbank, after a city in Los Angeles County we passed by on our way home shortly after we got him as a puppy. We both believed Burbank was more intelligent than many people we knew. We talked to our canine as though he was a person, and he became known among our friends as the *human-dog*.

Burbank was a black English labrador. He truly understood us and did almost everything we said. And we never trained him; there was no need. We traveled everywhere with him in the back of our car—Burbank sitting upright, crossing his front legs, and bracing against the front seat to keep his equilibrium as a person might.

Charlie and I thought no other dog would ever replace Burbank. We mourned his death as part of our family, and waited four years before even thinking of getting another animal. As time passed, though, the house felt empty without a wagging tail around, so we started searching for a canine once again.

The basic requirements were young, male, mixed breed, part labrador, and of large size but also different enough from Burbank that he wouldn't remind us of our former *human-dog*. After a couple of months, an image of a pup surfaced on the Net: it matched all our wishes.

The ad came from a small rescue center in Antelope Valley, at the western tip of the Mojave Desert and about an hour's car ride outside Los Angeles. The woman greeting us in the local supermarket's parking lot had three mutts in the back of her truck, all filthy and stinking of manure and hay. Two black puppies splashed with white, and a white one with cow-looking dark spots and a rosy, round tummy.

Genghis is the exact opposite of Burbank: mostly snow-white instead of pitch-black; lean instead of stocky; short, bristly hair instead of a slightly curly, longer coat; clumsy instead of graceful; pigheaded instead of agreeable; scared of his own shadow instead of courageous.

On the brain aptitude of Genghis, though, Charlie and I still disagree.

• • •

In support of his argument, my husband reminds me of a Genghis adventure from a year back: Along US Route 550, we have just passed the Santa Fe National Forest and Cuba, a village in Sandoval County, New Mexico. Population 735.

For the last few hours, our mutt has been busy standing on the back seat and scanning for cows. On my voice command of "Cow left!" or "Cow right!" Genghis turns toward the indicated open window to view and smell the cattle grazing on the plains. On road trips, nothing mesmerizes Genghis more than cows. But at the intersection with Route 96, he pokes his muzzle up next to our faces, and makes a drawn-out "*Mmmooowww*," followed five seconds later by a second "*Mmmooowww*." Translation: "I need to pee. Now!!!"

Genghis rarely asks to stop during car rides, but when he does, he means it!

The 550 is busy, livestock fences running both sides of the highway make it difficult to pull off, and our dog is growing impatient.

" Dirt road on the left!" I yell, as Charlie brakes suddenly to make the turn.

A forest service road parallels the Arroyo Chijuillita between open meadows and woods. As a cloud of dust rises behind us, Genghis readies himself to zoom out the door.

"Perfect timing," Charlie states, watching our mutt relieving himself for a good full minute.

"No kidding," I reply. "I am going to stretch my legs a bit. . . . "

A massive, vibrant orange, dome-shaped boulder stands a hundred feet ahead of me. I climb up from the backside with Genghis in tow. On top and at the edge of the cliff where I stop, a couple of twisted ponderosas protrude from the bare sandstone. Below me, the thriving shady forest of pine trees. Sand. Rocks. Water. And a matchstick-sized Charlie.

I hug my dog and shout "Charlieeeeee," so he can join us for a glimpse of this astonishing scenery.

As Genghis hears me yell my husband's name, he wriggles away from me and runs to the edge of the cliff. At full speed.

"Gengo, noooooooooooooo!" I scream. But it's too late. My dog doesn't listen. He has already reached the rim and I see his body flying off against the cerulean sky. Over twenty feet down.

Bewildered, I run toward the bluff. Charlie, who has observed the scene from below, runs toward Genghis. Or what's left of him. As I look over the rim's edge, my heart pounds fast, expecting to spot a white fur carpet splattered in a pool of blood.

But Genghis gets up, wags his tail, and closes the distance

between he and Charlie to say hello as though nothing happened. I am stunned.

"Is he okay?" I shout from the top of the dome, still expecting to see our dog collapse to the ground.

Charlie carefully inspects legs, paws, back, tail, belly, neck, and head. No blood. "He seems fine. . . ," I hear him say as I scamper down the cliff.

Now, we are both scrutinizing Genghis for signs of broken bones. "We need to take him to a vet somewhere," I say, aware that we are in the middle of nowhere. On a weekend.

Genghis loves unlooked-for attention. He darts upwards to lick my face—this time not to get a taste of what I ate—then lays down, turning belly-up for some extra scratches. When we are done, he sprints into the woods, running fast until he's panting, tongue dangling wide like a ladle.

Back in the car, the flying dog returns to his cow-sighting duties. His ears flop in the hot wind of US Route 550. He is blissful. He is okay.

• • •

No doubt, my dog is clueless about the surrounding environment and, yes, he doesn't respond well to orders. The cliff-jumping incident has not helped make my case for Genghis's brain acuity with Charlie. Yet, I still believe the ability to learn and obey our human commands is not the only measurement of intelligence for Genghis, or any dog. Understanding and respecting the independent wits of nonhuman animals can begin with paying attention to those who live most closely alongside us, and seeing them on their own terms, not just in how well they learn *human.*

It's hard to test canine acumen, just as it is with our intellect. Individual dogs—not only breeds—differ wildly in their personalities. As we do. But Genghis can read our cues, pay attention to the words of our speech (not just the tone), solve spatial problems, and show emotions like love, jealousy, and much more.

Now, housebound and with spare time to observe his demeanor in even more detail, I am further aware of Genghis's capabilities and potentials.

Genghis may not be a super-dog able to comprehend up to 250 words, and he may seem oblivious when it comes to his environs—but he is not stupid. Rather, he is an independent-minded, stubborn, unwilling-to-follow-orders type of canine. He knows what he wants and how to get it (often by disarming us with his charm). My dog is a con artist.

At the end of the day, it doesn't matter if Charlie and I argue about Genghis's intellect. With all his idiosyncrasies and his either large or small brain, he conquered not only our home but also our hearts.

• • •

Genghis's love and goofiness also helped me cope with uncertain times in my life. The symbiotic bond between our two species is not something I can scientifically explain. It goes beyond reason because love itself has little to do with rationality. What I do know is that Genghis strikes a profound emotional cord with me. He can get me off the couch and help me focus on something other than my own tribulations; he can push me to reconnect with the outside world, to breathe the air and smell the grass.

I remember one day, at the end of the third month of the pandemic. By then it was clear that I would not be going back to Italy to visit my family any time soon. Leaving Europe and moving with Charlie to the States has been one of the best decisions I have ever made. I miss my family back in the Umbrian countryside, but I am happy here. And I know that as soon as I feel homesick, I can hop on a plane and return to the motherland. Except for when an unpredicted pandemic abruptly changed the situation. Ninety days after the virus entered our quotidian existence, I was heartbroken about not being able to see my octogenarian parents, and for the likelihood of not traveling for the foreseeable future.

Something I never do is lie down in bed during the day,

unless I am sick. That morning, though, I went to the bedroom, pulled the blanket up over my head, and lay on my side, feeling detached and thinking about my distant loved ones.

10:00 a.m. is when I typically walk my dog in the neighborhood. He knows it, and if I forget about it, he is sure to remind me. But not that day. Instead of complaining or scratching my leg to get attention, he jumped on the bed. Slowly, and with unusual restraint, he placed himself next to me. My chin touched his head, and the soft fur of his ear tickled my nose.

Genghis adjusted himself even closer to me by pushing his back and butt into my belly and upper legs. In fetal position, I pulled one arm from under the blanket and held his front paw in my hand. As I clenched it a little, my pup responded by squeezing back. We embraced and held paws. It was a good feeling. A warm one. Genghis was not asking me to go out. He was not whining. He was not his goofy self. My dog was there for me. Silently. Selflessly. As long as I needed him to be.

Not only wild animals, but domestic ones as well, can offer relief during taxing periods of our lives. There is an intangible kinship with the creatures we welcome in our homes, being they cats, dogs, bunnies, or teacup pigs. We impact each other profoundly.

Dogs understand us more than we think. They recognize when we are sad or sick and when we need them the most.

Dogs are enthralling to watch up close, providing us with an infinite source of little discoveries. Dogs give us distractions, laughs, and joy.

Dogs make us feel good.

5

THROUGH GENGHIS'S EYES

10:00 a.m.: Genghis is sitting next to me, carefully noting every movement of my body. My hands are furiously typing, but his inside clock is telling him it's time for the daily stroll.

10:02 a.m.: Still typing.

"*Tappetino!*" I say in Italian, telling him to go back to his pink flamingo–covered bed. Yeah, my dog is not only shrewd; he is also bilingual.

Genghis goes back to his cot with an unmistakable grunt of frustration and disappointment.

10:05 a.m.: Still writing. My pup is back, sitting next to me. His paw delicately touches my leg once, then less gracefully the second time. He's growing impatient about my posture that doesn't alter. Now, he scratches my arm and I turn slightly to find his large wet nose almost next to my cheek. There is no chance I can finish what I am doing. We look at each other and I smile. His tail wags. He knows he's won.

I put Genghis in his collar and leash and don my own antivirus muzzle. We are out the door for another walk in the neighborhood. Today, to be original, we will head south then east instead of north then west. My hound is fond of the idea and he speeds up toward the first patch of grass. As he stops to savor some unknown but surely delightful smell on a neighbor's lawn, I adjust the mask that, once again, is sliding down my nose.

My mobile phone rings and Genghis looks up with a new sign of disapproval. He is not fond of interruptions during our strolls because it means I am not fully paying attention to him. I don't enjoy disruptions either. I savor this time to experience LA on foot, instead of behind the wheel of a car running around frenetically. I love to walk, observe, and let my mind meander any place it wishes to go. Still no coyotes around today.

I am now phone-free, and he glares at my face wondering if we are finally ready to proceed as we should. I nod and smile again, proud of this two-way silent communication that has grown between us during our years together.

For the first time since the pandemic started, though, I realize Genghis can't see my mouth, or most of my face, when we walk. This morning, with dark hat, oversized sunglasses, and a black mask, I look more like Darth Vader than his usual chaperone. What might my dog think of this new disguise? Is Genghis aware of it? Can he still read the subtle changes of my facial muscles that imply a smile?

• • •

I just read a newly published paper in the *Journal of Neuroscience* about how dog minds are not hardwired to respond to human facial expressions. Based on the authors' experiment, our furry companions don't seem to have a brain "designed" for focusing on our faces, and they can't tell the difference between the back and the front of our heads.

Charlie, who often calls Genghis *Noodle-Brain*, would probably agree with them. . . .

Having studied animal behavior (though marine mammals, not terrestrial ones, are my forte), some conclusions of this paper sounded odd. Perhaps it's because when it comes to my four-legged best friend, my judgment might be less than objective. Maybe it's because I have spent such a long time in the company of dogs that I find it hard to believe they don't recognize human facial expressions.

So, back from my walk, I take a few hours to dig a little deeper and see what other scientific literature has to say about these canines and human expressions.

The question of whether dogs—and other animals—respond to our faces has been the focus of a lot of research over the last decade. Several scientific investigations run contrary to the new study I'd read in the *Journal of Neuroscience*, and seem to have convincingly proven that domestic canines do, in fact, discriminate between positive and negative facial expressions of humans. In particular, a couple of studies showed how dogs can distinguish an angry from a happy human face, finding the angry one "aversive." Research has also suggested that pooches do indeed have separate regions of their brains for processing our facial expressions.

As often happens in science, there is still controversy on the topic, but most investigations favor dogs being able to recognize and make large use of our facial language.

Reading all available literature confirmed what I had previously thought, especially as someone who has spent almost fifty years alongside dogs. To me, it's not surprising to think these animals pick up on our visage, considering we don't have expressive tails or ears. Dogs utilize and compile many cues from different senses to better grasp what we do and feel at any given moment, and our facial emoticon is a likely part of the cocktail.

• • •

So, is Genghis behaving differently now that I wear a mask during our walks?

As I reflect on this seemingly naive question, it's mind-boggling to me what we still don't know about our best friends, even if they are our shadows twenty-four-seven. I realize now that, hectic as I always was in my prepandemic life, I haven't invested much time in observing Genghis, nor learning from what he had to "say."

It took a stay-at-home order to force me to slow down my pace, to stop tickling a computer keyboard around the clock, to get up from my office chair and start quietly noting Genghis's circadian habits and his physical and vocal reactions to the surrounding environment and other animals. Me included.

As I'd done in my research on whales and dolphins for so many years, I began to pose more questions and look for answers.

• • •

After closely eyeing Genghis for a while and watching his reactions, I haven't spotted any behavioral differences at all whether or not I wear a mask during our strolls. And honestly, I don't remember any difference in his behavior when we donned our Covid muzzles for the first time.

There has been no breakdown in our communication, not with me nor with anyone we meet.

Are my body language, smell, voice, and conduct during these walks so familiar to Genghis that he doesn't need to evaluate what's behind my mask to make judgments? Am I talking more to him now that I wear a mask and don't even realize it? Or, once again, is he the eternal *Noodle-Brain* that my husband says he is, and nothing matters to him?

Doing some literature research on this specific topic doesn't help. Not surprising given that the last time we covered our faces while walking on the street was during the 1918 influenza pandemic—not a period in history in which scientists were engrossed with learning about dogs' reactions to masks.

• • •

Almost concurrently with my opportunistic experiments with Genghis on the streets of Los Angeles, Marc Bekoff, a colleague of mine in Colorado and a renowned aficionado of dog behavior, is asking similar questions about hounds and masks.

Walking in a park in Boulder, one can't miss Marc; he spends nearly all day, almost every day, frequenting the city's dog parks. With gray-blondish hair tied in a long ruffled ponytail, silver earring (just one), T-shirt, and rolled-up jeans, he is the only person who can pass a full eight hours observing dogs' deeds with no break, except maybe for a swift vegan meal.

Marc started wondering how domestic pets would respond to masked human faces when he began receiving messages from local folks asking these questions. At first, he replied that he had no idea. Well aware of the dissimilarities in dogs' personalities, and how different guardians affect their canine companions' behaviors, Marc figured it would be difficult to draw any generalized conclusions about the impacts of masks. Of a curious type, though, he left no stone unturned.

And so it goes that, midpandemic, Marc decided to perform a citizen science experiment, collecting data from people and pets whom he randomly encountered in his hometown of Boulder. If there is a person on Earth well-versed in citizen science, it's undoubtedly Marc.

He asked owners how their dogs responded to them wearing a mask, but he also gathered notes on how other people's pups interacted with him while he was wearing a mask. Like mine, his research wasn't a strictly scientific endeavor; it was just Marc being inquisitive and trying to shed some light on canine reactions to this eerie time we live in.

Based on one hundred interviews, a good percentage of dogs seemed slightly more hesitant to approach masked people, tending to stare at and inspect mask-wearing humans for a longer period. There was also more sniffing the air. Of course, this made perfect sense going back to how dogs use signals from different senses to better comprehend what's going on in their surroundings.

When a masked Marc approached some of the dogs he knew personally, prior to COVID-19 (here, the number of samples is particularly low), they tended to be a little bit more alert from a distance, gaining more confidence as he approached and spoke to them. But there wasn't a decisive conclusion to draw from his trial.

While Marc and I were engaged in our opportunistic investigations, other scientists worldwide began conducting similar in-the-neighborhood experiments with their pets and those of friends and acquaintances. The results were similar, with more dogs showing no significant reaction to humans with masks.

• • •

In the end, it probably boils down to different personalities. For Genghis, who still behaves like an inquisitive puppy despite his eight years of age, there is so much to do during our walks; so many trees and grass patches to sniff; so many things to see, chase after, and cower from.

The new normal perhaps feels a lot like the old normal to my mutt, and my mask doesn't make a hint of a difference.

In his mind, the global pandemic just means more daily strolls.

For me, it's a shot at better grasping what happens on the other side of the leash, when I let go of my alpha status by scampering into my dog's paws, muting my phone, and reconnecting to that core curiosity that has driven my career in ecology.

6

THE REMEDIAL GARDEN

As early as I can remember, in all the postage-stamp-sized balconies and modest backyards that we had in the various Italian homes of my childhood (we moved a lot), my mom invariably tended to flowers, vegetables, and herbs. Our blossoming gardens were the envy of the neighborhood, and our friends used my mother as a human-flora-encyclopedia for advice on how to grow their own.

Even now, at eighty-five years of age and with rampant arthritis, she works daily in her large hillside backyard in the Umbrian countryside. She devotes hours to the company of her green offspring, caring for them with meticulous kindness. She pots up seedlings, uproots weeds, and harvests what nature gives back to her.

One can smell her countless species of flowers from down the street, glimpse bourgeoning bushes of roses and lavender, and watch her picking the leaves of sage growing in small terracotta pots near the gate, or kneeling near the blankets of arugula and clumps of red tomatoes in her opulent vegetable patch. Last summer, a vehement and unexpected storm hit her backyard, destroying most of her plants and decimating the vegetable garden. She called me in tears, as if she had lost her most precious jewels.

In and outside of her home, luscious, vibrantly painted orchids adorn every corner. Their shapes remind me more of animals than blossoms. She loves them madly.

"What would you like for your birthday?" my dad asks mom every year. Her response is always the same. "An orchid."

I love my mother's unfading passion for gardening, but I never thought I had green thumb potential. I was wrong. She did pass along some verdant genes after all, and during the uncertainty and isolation of the pandemic, gardening turned out to be a great form of relief, having a soothing, therapeutic effect on my mind.

• • •

My rental house on the bluffs of Los Angeles has a good-sized front and backyard. Now, some people call this city a desert while others argue that, technically, LA has more of a Mediterranean climate, with hot, dry summers and mild winters. Either way, when it does rain, it doesn't rain much.

I think it's a good idea to consider LA as more of a desert because, no matter what, water is an extremely precious resource here, and consequently, it doesn't hurt to conserve it. We might need it for the next wildfire.

When my husband and I moved into our rental, we inherited the typical suburban garden. Like many homes in the neighborhood, our backyard was made up of a large, relentlessly thirsty lawn, rose bushes, begonias, and many species of flowers, all of which need lots of water. And for the icing on the cake, there were extensive ferns and irises, more plants known to be water guzzlers.

As spring turned into summer, with H_2O preservation in mind and relishing the South Cali weather, I decided to give the yard a face-lift.

Replacing the entire lawn was at the top of my list, but the landlord wouldn't have taken that well (or at least, that's what I thought), so I decided to do it gradually. As I write these words, I am still making the lawn disappear a slice at a time. And with his blessing.

My second goal was to use only native, low-maintenance plants with little need for water and organic mulch to reduce weeds, so they wouldn't compete with the other plants for water. In my mind, having a drought-resistant garden never meant having a less appealing yard.

Finding native, desert-friendly plants required some research of the local flora on my part; fortunately, research is something I can do. The low-maintenance aspect was necessary because I knew I would not be able to keep up with the garden. My green thumb would only go so far once I returned to full-time work, back on the ocean studying dolphins and whales, now stalled for lack of funding.

I had a third and final rule for my backyard project. It needed to be realized on a carbon-zero budget, meaning I decided to recycle everything, from terracotta pots to mulch, from plants to flagstones. Nextdoor turned out to be the solution to my sustainable, no-waste project. I just needed to steer clear of engaging in futile online Nextdoorian chats about decimating local coyotes or slowing traffic by adding more speed bumps in our streets.

With these constraints in mind, I joined the online Nextdoor Succulent Lovers Group, organized by a retired travel executive and succulent guru of Kentwood, the suburb where I live. He also happened to be one of the most active members of Nextdoor, with 464 posts (equally divided between succulent advice and daily jokes), 1,418 replies, and 12,564 thanks and welcomes. Not bad for a retired executive.

From that group, I expanded my daily online search to explore the free "garden" sections of Nextdoor and Craigslist, looking for neighbors who were getting rid of anything that could fit my gardening plans. I learned there is no limit to what one can source for a backyard, from six-foot-tall cacti to Italian terracotta crocks, from slate slabs to shrubs of lavender and Arroyo lupine. All of this without venturing outside of a three-mile radius from home.

Six months after my garden mission was fully operative, our landlord came to drop something off. Honestly, I was nervous.

"What if he hates it?" Charlie asked, not helping me to feel better.

"Well, I will deal with that," I responded. "We are definitely using less water now. . . . Plus, my orphan plants are strong and resilient," I added. Charlie glanced at me, raising his eyebrows, not too confident in my selling points.

I walked outside, waiting for the landlord. Little was left of his original backyard. My urban succulent jungle had taken over, with a vengeance! Spiky and rough, soft and velvety, gigantic and minuscule, phallic and globose, dark green and light pea toned, sought after and familiar, hip and exotic, toxic and harmless, straight like spaghetti and pleated like kilts. It was a green heaven. At least, for me.

The landlord parked his night-blue Tesla in front of the house. He stepped out of the car, tall and skinny as I'd last remembered him. After taking off his sunglasses and adjusting his close-cropped salt and pepper hair, he looked around. I waited for the hammer to fall. . . .

"Wow, Maddalena," he said with a smile before I could even say hello, "what a difference! This is great! I love it! Did you do it all by yourself?"

"Hi, and yes, thank you!" I responded, relieved. "It's low-maintenance, requires little water . . . and it's a work-in-process," I added, thinking I still needed to defend my actions.

We walked through the entire unrecognizable backyard, stepping on rosy flagstones over the few leftover patches of familiar grass.

"Please feel free to do whatever you wish," he said before saying goodbye and heading back to his Tesla. "Big fan of your work, on the water with dolphins, and here too!"

Back inside, I zoomed into Charlie's office. "He liked it! I can do more! I got his blessing!" My husband smiled and said, "Great for you! Now you won't have to dig up all the plants."

• • •

Getting my hands dirty digging holes, sowing seeds, and tucking roots into the soil of my secondhand garden turned out to be an antidote for my body and mind.

I discovered that working the soil was more than just excavating and potting. Gardening allowed me to lose myself for a time in a universe of my own making. I can see why my quintessential garden-wizard mother cherishes her green offspring. When I visit her, I can understand her pride in taking me on a tour of the blossoming white, purple, and striped lilies, in handpicking the first leaves of *Valeriana* after a chilly winter, the sun-kissed, pulpy tomatoes, and the flowers of calendula, "*belle* in salads and *buonissime* for making a yellow-dyed *risotto*," as she reminds me.

Now, my backyard is a safe place to be alone and at peace while the world around me roils in uncertainty. Even an anxious brain like mine, not prone to sitting still in meditation, on occasion needs some reprieve from stress.

And it was no surprise for me to learn of gardening's reparative powers, both in historical and contemporary mental-health treatments. Nature, even in a pocket-sized green plot, offers a great escape from human troubles during difficult times, and we can find the wild all around us if we only choose to see it.

The natural world is where our human instincts tell us to retreat when life is hard.

Walking Genghis in the neighborhood gets me out the door and helps satisfy my sense of curiosity. I observe the urban bestiary at my disposal, develop questions, search for answers, then come up with new questions. I am at ease and worry-free. But my scientist's white coat is still on.

Gardening is different. Plants have taught me how to switch gears entirely and change the pace of things. They have taught me how to take off the white coat and empty my mind. Even if tending a garden has little to do with observing large wild animals, both require time and patience. I learned how to stop and smell the roses. Or the Queens of the Night, to be precise.

When two Queens blossomed in my backyard, their beauty took my breath away. Formally known as *Epiphyllum oxypetalum*, this exotic orchid cactus (of the genus *Cereus*) has been on my wish list since my carbon-zero horticulture project launched. Perhaps unconsciously it reminded me of my mother's orchids back home.

And one day, *poof*, there it was, on Nextdoor: an image of not just one Queen, but a couple of them, resting on a mound of Mexican fenceposts (columnar cacti with pleated ribs that can grow up to twenty feet tall). All sitting at the curb and waiting for the trash truck!

The post under the picture read "FREE—cacti cuttings. If interested, message to pick up." *G.F.,* I *hr ago,* 0.9 *miles, Kentwood North, June* 3.

Promptly, I wrote back, "Dear G.F., Would it be okay if I come by and pick up a Queen of the Night and a few of your other cacti for my yard? I live less than a mile away. I can come now. Thank you. Sincerely, Maddalena."

"Please take them all, here's my address! Smiley Face Emoji! Sparkling Heart Emoji! Triple Cactus Emoji!!!" was G's speedy reply.

Dropping whatever I was doing, I drove to the address with garden gloves, newspapers, a mask, and a cutter. Just in case. An hour and three car trips later, two Queens of the Night and fifteen Mexican fenceposts, spanning from one to six feet tall, were piled up in our driveway. Within two days, I planted all the fenceposts in the soil of our back and front yards, along with the green strip near the street. A couple of recycled terracotta pots with drain holes were reserved for my Queens. I placed them in a shady corner with other plants, knowing that these climbing cacti—natives of Central America—tend to live as epiphytes. Meaning: they need help from fellow plants to flourish.

Once done, I gazed at my Nextdoor-built garden with pride, learning the lesson that more can come from Nextdoorians than just gossip, and that connecting with my local community can be a very good thing. The towery Mexican fenceposts were breaking the monotony of the low-to-the-ground succulent backdrop, providing a more three-dimensional feeling. But the two Queens of the Night fascinated me the most. Their flowers, growing from fleshy stems, last one night only; they open when the sun sets and wilt when it rises. And that magic typically happens only once a year.

I waited a long time for the flowers of my Queens to bloom. And when the time finally came, I watched three blushing, artichoke-like buds dangle from the long stems. I waited for the crooked blossoms to unfurl and for the pink-tipped sepals to peel. Unhurriedly. At dusk, the glowing flowers began to open. And as the dark of the night descended, the creamy-white, waxy petals—arranged in the form of a cup—revealed themselves, opening the door to the delicate, pale-yellow, skinny stamens on the inside. It was hard to miss these flowers even in the deepest darkness: their pungent, sweet-scented fragrance saturated the air like a freshly baked vanilla cake.

Three palm-sized flowers were spectacular enough for me to see. A bloom *en masse* in a single night has to be an *Alice in Wonderland* experience.

The story goes that during the Great Depression, in Jackson, Mississippi, writer Eudora Welty and her artistic friends—in honor of this cactus—founded the Night-Blooming Cereus Club. In anticipation of the unison debut of their nocturnal cereuses, these Southern ladies would gather to witness the spectacle, talk poetry and jazz, and drink sweet tea in the heat of the midsummer night. Aptly, the club motto, slightly altered from a Rudy Vallée song, was: "Don't take it cereus; life's too mysterious." It was a call to good fellowship, a reminder to savor life on Earth and what nature has to offer in harsh times; and those of the Great Depression were harsh, indeed.

But the night blooming of this ephemeral flower is not theater; it's not a performance staged for human amusement. It's a strategy: When other plants sleep, there is less competition for pollinators. Simply put, night blooming equals a better chance for this species' survival.

I imagine Eudora and her friends sitting around the garden and sipping tea, the explosion of flowers, the potent smell. I envision the Queens of the Night secretly communicating with each other to bloom in unison. Without brain, without intent or experience, yet with great precision and efficacy.

Animals are not the only organisms capable of "talking." Plants, too, are social and can exchange information and share resources by secreting chemicals in the soil or releasing volatile organic compounds into the air. They don't communicate as we do. Nor as dolphins, chimps, or birds do. Plants do it silently and secretively, for eons. They send and receive signals constantly. And we are only now learning how to eavesdrop.

By the crack of dawn, the private spectacle of my Queens

of the Night was over. Their short-lived blossoms were shut, flaccidly hanging down like teeny chickens twisted by their necks. These ephemeral beauties and their pungent smell were gone.

Nothing lasts but the memory.

• • •

Even before I started tending my own garden, plants like cacti, succulents, orchids, roses, and tulips have never been décor to me. They are alive, sensitive beings. Though I study animals, I am drawn to the cyclical, transient nature of plants. Their covert communication. The productivity they symbolize as they grow.

Devoting hours to my backyard, with only the company of Genghis, the squirrels, and the hummingbirds sucking on the newly planted flowers of the lupine, is also a way for me to be close to my mother. Working in the garden, I feel her presence when looking for the ideal spot to plant a salvaged blue agave or one more Mexican fencepost found at the curbside. I can hear her voice telling me to be careful with the poisonous pencil cactus I am touching with my bare hands.

Thousands of miles away and an ocean apart, she is beside me.

7

WASP ON AVOCADO TOAST

Multigrain bread well-toasted, smashed avocado, a pinch of salt, several thin slices of fresh radish, topped with a few sprigs of cilantro.

Ready to eat my healthful lunch in the garden, I open my mouth to enjoy the first bite when, all of a sudden and a little out of focus for the proximity, an extra garnish with a mustard-yellow and black body hovers just a few inches from my nose.

A paper wasp has landed on my toast.

The compound eyes, each a cluster of thousands of small, telescope-like units, are facing me as the slender, orange legs try to move while slightly sinking into the green mud of the avocado. For a moment, we both stop our activities startled by this very personal encounter.

I slowly put my toast back on the plate as the wasp reaches the edge of the avocado, walks on the hard, white surface of a radish slice, and then takes off like a miniature plane, with a bit of muck still glued to its frame.

I follow this slender, narrow-waisted insect with my eyes as it flies circles around the toast with its six long, spindly orange legs dangling below the body. I am not fearful of being stung. This kind of wasp is not aggressive and won't sting unless I provoke it or accidentally disturb its colony, often built in human-made structures.

Paper wasps are different from their next of kin, the more belligerent yellow jacket, another common visitor to my yard. The yellow jacket has a dissimilar color pattern to the paper wasp, dumpier frame, and smaller legs it keeps tucked under its body while airborne. And it's typically a yellow jacket, not a paper wasp, that lands on my lunch or goes for a swim in my soda when I am not looking.

Instead of probing for flowers, the yellow jacket favors protein sources; although their stings are used to paralyze their prey—usually other insects—there have been a few times I got a taste of them myself while gardening. It's only the females, though, that are equipped with a modified egg-laying organ able to pump one or more doses of venom into my skin.

Most of us are scared of wasps, but it's astonishing that of thousands of species hovering in the States, few are potentially dangerous to humans and only a handful are considered pests. And although both paper wasps and yellow jackets are second-rate pollinators because they don't have the fuzzy bodies of their cousins, the bees, to which pollen tends to stick, they do still help the environment by eating nectar and spreading pollen.

• • •

The paper wasp is now resting on my wood table with its smoky black wings folded lengthwise, and I can now see, from her hefty size, that she is likely a female.

As I finally enjoy the first bite of toast, I follow the antics of this unappreciated insect, definitely more intriguing than the book I was planning to read.

After a short break, my wasp is back in the air, this time heading toward the lounge chair under the shade of the Chinese strawberry tree. I track her movements as she stops outside a tubular gap created by the red Sunbrella fabric covering the vertical part of the teak.

Quietly, I move closer, but not too close, to observe a seemingly secret wasp meeting. As if they were soldiers standing guard, my wasp—and another one next to her—stand still, securing the entrance of the fissure.

Every few minutes, a few wasps leave, and some return,

like participants at a tedious conference craving a coffee break. On and off, I see the Avocado-Toast wasp, renamed AT, engaging with one of the arriving participants, just before this member enters the open gate between the heavy sheets of fabric. At this point, with all the coming and going, the only way I can still discern AT from the other wasps is because of that smear of avocado still glued to her body.

I can't discern what's going on inside that dark room hidden in my lounge chair's frame, but I am pretty sure there is a nest, and AT is at work as one of the entry guards.

A guard wasp can be very defensive of her nest. If AT suddenly decides I am an invader instead of an avocado-toast provider and stings me, her venom will instantly release a sort of alarm-signaling odor. This smell is strong enough to be picked up by other workers in the colony; it's a bell advertising that danger is in the air, and all the laborers, filled with their venom reservoirs, will quickly swarm in defense of their nest. . . . And I know I don't want to be around to see that.

Slowly, I go inside to pick up the binoculars I use to spot dolphins and whales from the deck of my research boat, and then return to the yard, moving my chair farther away from the nest to continue my observations as a spectator in an open theater.

• • •

These social wasps, living in highly organized colonies, build intricate, small nests of a papery substance (hence the name "paper"), molded from wood fibers that females have scraped with their powerful mandibles from tree bark, fence posts, or anything woody in their surroundings, and then chewed with saliva to form a meatball-like, pulpy paste.

The final structure is an architectural wonder in the shape of an upside-down umbrella supported by a single stalk or an open honeycomb; a piece of art that's at the same time strong and unbelievably light in weight. These urban-engineered sheltered nests, in which wasps lay eggs and take care of their young, are predictably built under roof eaves, and every so often . . . inside gashes of lawn furniture such as my lounge chair!

• • •

AT continues her occasional networking with other wasps in transit, moving her tiny antennae. These little orange probes are handy to gather all sorts of information from the nearby environment, friend and enemy presences included.

Every one of these wasps knows its place in society: the fertile queens lay the eggs and the unfertile workers, well . . . work. And the making of a queen starts early on in this particular species.

Like bottlenose dolphins—and contrarily from other

social insects—paper wasps live in somewhat flexible and fluid societies. In their waspy word, though, society works differently than for my ocean companions.

Social insects typically have distinct classes that are determined at birth. But not paper wasps; their societies are more elastic and they often have only three castes: males, infertile female workers (making up most of the wasps in a nest during summertime), and queens. This is a good thing for females because any one of them can climb the social ladder to occupy the queen's throne; young queens often leave the nest to reproduce and form their own colonies. But usually, the little busy workers relinquish breeding in exchange for nest protection duties and to help raise their egg-white, leg-less larva siblings. It's these workers that leave the nest in search of food and will sting if they have the feeling there is a threat around. Like me.

If I were born a paper wasp, I would hope to be a female because female workers have a say over males. They not only wrestle, bite, and sting workers from the opposite sex but also stuff them, head first, into empty nest cells as if they were ingredients in a muffin pan. The reason for this aggressive behavior is to keep males from eating the provisions needed by the more vital developing larvae, which—ultimately—will become the colony's next reproducing generation.

• • •

I observe AT as she continues to defend her entrance, interacting here and there with the incoming and outgoing flow of other workers. It seems farfetched to think that paper wasps, despite a brain less than a millionth the size of mine, are socially adept, but it's true. So much so, in fact, that some queens can identify other wasps in the colony by their unique facial patterns. Although all wasps may appear the same to us, they have distinctive markings on their heads that allow for visual ID.

We humans can recognize each other's faces, and many other vertebrates can recognize each other too, at least at some levels and in some circumstances. I think about how I can photo-identify individual bottlenose dolphins from the notches on their dorsal fins, and how even the unique facial features of these marine mammals can be used as a complemental tool to distinguish one another. But insects? Facial recognition is certainly not something that comes to mind when one sees a wasp nearby. And it's not a trait shared by all paper wasps either; the only ones endowed with this talent of learning faces seem to be the *Polistes fuscatus*, which always live in colonies with more than one queen.

When you have only one ruler, like in a bee colony, things are easy: there is a queen and everyone else knows its role in the community. When a communal society has more than one sovereign, as happens in some paper wasp colonies that can easily count more than five queens in a single nest, things can get complicated. And it's here that their evolved ability to recognize faces helps the multiple rulers negotiate with each other. In the struggle for the ultimate throne, queens not only fight other potential rulers but, by recognizing the faces of their adversaries, they can keep track of those they have already defeated and those whom they have been defeated by. This hierarchy will usually end up with a dominant queen that produces most of the offspring and a few subordinate queens, which either stay, laying fewer eggs than the dominant queen, or leave the colony to build their own smaller, less sturdy nests somewhere else.

Over time, the specialized and shrewd face-learning knack of these wasps can extend to every individual in the nest. It's something that has evolved in the last few thousand years, not to catch prey or survive climate change, but to become better and cleverer at dealing with each other.

Individual recognition, known as the most complex form of recognition, requires flexible learning and memory—not something one expects from a tiny wasp. Not even a queen.

• • •

AT has left her post at the entrance of the colony.

I spotted her walking inside the cranny and disappearing into the black hole of the lounge chair a few minutes ago. I wait a little longer just in case she comes back out, but another avocado-less wasp seems to have already taken up her guard position.

I finally give up and take my binoculars, book, and empty plate, and head inside to my own nest.

8

CAPTIVE ANIMALS

I am an animal in captivity. Or at least I feel so during this surreal period of my life.

It's been several months now since I've been out on the water with my research crew. And I miss the dolphins, the whales, and the vastness of the ocean.

When I first began my investigations of their behavior many years ago, I knew these creatures primarily as the objects of my research. Still, as time passed, I came to distinguish them as single individuals, and not merely for the unique notches on their dorsal fins; also for their cognitive abilities, for their personalities and emotions.

At sea, I began to recognize some of them by sight, and

like my human friends, they became an integral part of my life. I learned of their needs, not only for space but also for companionship. And I witnessed their fluid, complex societies, which, in many ways, are similar to our own, for good and for ill.

Now that I find myself caged within the four walls of my suburban home, I have ample time to think about the dolphins swimming free in the ocean, and also those confined in small tanks around the world.

I have seen dolphins behind the glass of an enclosure, swimming in endless circles, chewing the walls, their skin burned by the sun. I have witnessed disturbing patterns of behavior repeating themselves in an unceasing cycle, sometimes accompanied by chronic health issues. I have observed first-hand the very different lives of animals detained in aquaria and marine parks versus those in the wild. And these days, more than ever, I cannot help wondering why anyone (except those who profit from it) would think it's a good idea to keep these mammals in captivity.

In my line of work, I've heard all kind of excuses and reasons for enclosing dolphins in tanks; the most frequent being education, conservation, and research.

To whomever asks me about the learning value of taking a child to a marine park, I would say it is far from being an educational experience because the child doesn't see or understand what these animals truly are. Jumping on command or catching a ball tossed from the hand of a trainer during a performance is stereotyped, clown-esque behavior.

Imprisoning dolphins—and I would stretch this to include many other creatures—may have been more acceptable decades ago, when we didn't know any better; when we didn't have enough information about who these animals are in the wild and what they need to thrive. But today, we know a lot more than we did back then, and we have an informed responsibility to make ethical and compassionate decisions.

Now we know that dolphins are large-brained, sentient animals. Deprived of their natural space, dolphins experience clear psychological and physical damage.

• • •

If we consider our species the pinnacle of intelligence, dolphins rank just behind us, scoring even higher than their great ape cousins. Dolphins can process complex information because their brains have an intricate and developed neocortex compared to other beings, including humans. Bonus: they are blessed with spindle-shaped neurons, the *Von Economo* neurons, which are vital for social cognition and have been linked—in our species—to an ability to "sense" what others are thinking.

There is no doubt that intelligence is difficult to define.

Looking into the animal world, almost any species may be considered smart depending on what definition of intelligence we decide to apply. I can make an excellent case for any of my dogs, Genghis included. But especially for dolphins, great apes, elephants, and our kind, brain complexity, social complexity, and ecological complexity are closely linked.

All this cognitive ability has allowed several dolphin species to develop fluid societies in which they can flourish against the backdrop of a challenging, three-dimensional, open liquid environment. Bottlenose dolphins, for instance, have flexible and remarkable social and communication skills. They thrive in networks characterized by highly differentiated relationships that often rely on precise memory of who owes who a favor and who is a true friend. They engage in cooperative hunting, and partition resources so that prey is shared throughout the group.

Even if I try, I can't remember how often have I seen teamwork in groups of dolphins and whales out on the ocean, it's so common.

• • •

I stare out the window of my home studio. As the lupine gently dances in the wind, my mind travels back, to many years before the pandemic seeped into our lives and the world changed.

I can't go anywhere, but my brain can, this time fetching

memories of the beauty, freedom, and synergy of the humpbacks off Alaska.

Chatham Strait. It's early on a midsummer morning. The sea surface sparkles like chrome. It's crisp and lake-like and yet unsculpted by the fingers of the wind. Dawn is peaceful, seeming more a subtle lightening of the sky than the transition from night to day. This time of year, the night is more an implied concept than visible reality.

Beneath the surface, a high-pitched *mooooooo* sound slowly morphs into something akin to a strident violin tone. One humpback whale talks. The others listen. Something is out of tune, different. This is not the harmonious whale song one might hear on some relaxation CD. It's not the song males chant to court females in mating season, nor is it a low-frequency sound that may travel thousands of miles. This is a different tune, a jarring noise of constant frequency. It's the call to feed.

As one leviathan hums the feeding call, other whales dive below a large shoal of herring and begin to blow strings of bubbles that ascend toward the surface, creating a cylindrical wall of shimmering spheres and sound. The humpbacks glide in a circular motion; bodies inclined inward, flippers aligned vertically in the water column. Their long pectoral "wings" allow increasingly tighter turns as they bank steeply, spiraling their bus-sized bodies upward toward the surface as the bubble net they have created contracts around their prey. Thousands of herring swirl and twist inside the curtain of bubbles, constantly reshaping their mass in response to the impending threat of predation. The humpbacks move their flippers as an airplane might adjust its wing flaps on the final landing approach. Then, flawlessly synchronized with almost military precision, the whales swim quickly toward the surface and through the center of the bubble net. Their mouths are wide open and extended, thanks to adaptations that enable their jaws to unhinge and their ventral pleats to unfold, allowing them to take in a vast volume of fish and water. As these massive animals surge and explode from the calm Chatham Strait, over a ton of water flows out through the baleen of their enormous mouths, leaving hundreds of herring trapped and ingested in a single gulp.

In the open ocean, cooperation is as crucial for the leviathan humpbacks of the cold Chatham Strait as it is for dolphins in my study area off California. Bottlenose dolphin males can form coalitions to sexually coerce females (at times acting quite violently) or defeat other male teams; females can help other females during labor and delivery of a newborn; individuals collaborate to feed or defend themselves against predators. Similar to us, and most other living beings in the wild, they rely on relationships to survive and flourish. And dolphins can care a great deal for each other . . . and for some humans too.

Aside from my personal experience with a pod of coastal bottlenose dolphins leading my research team and me to save a young girl from drowning, three miles off the coast of Malibu,* there are numerous anecdotes of these animals saving humans from death or adversity, and more discovered as days pass. These are accounts of dolphins guiding us to a safe shore, fending off sharks, or keeping us afloat until aid arrives.

In their ocean domain, mothers and calves have long-term solid, social bonds. A calf can spend two or more years next to its mother, understanding its place in the marine environment. Free-ranging dolphins play, bond, imitate, "talk," learn from each other, and transfer information from generation to generation. This ability to pass acquired behaviors to their progeny makes them cultural animals like us. And like us, they can recognize themselves as individuals; they are self-aware, even if the extent of dolphin self-awareness remains to be fully explored.

Dolphins are always on the move at sea, often traveling hundreds and hundreds of miles. They are essentially complex social mammals that need expansive space to live.

A tank can't even begin to address these needs.

---

* This account is narrated in my book *Dolphin Confidential: Confessions of a Field Biologist.*

It's hard for me, confined within the walls of my house, with fewer places to go and see, not to dwell on the claustrophobic lives of my captive ocean companions, the dolphins kept in the many aquaria around the world, and all the things they cannot experience in the open sea—the miles they can't travel, the families they have lost, the prey they can't hunt, the depths they can't explore. And because of us.

We like to think of dolphins as happy beings with an omnipresent smile frolicking in the wild or in a pool. We tend to anthropomorphize them, projecting our attributes onto them. But what many believe is the blissful face of a dolphin can obscure the animal's true feeling, especially when we keep them confined. Let's not forget that these dolphins, like many other caged species, are not in captivity to preserve genetic biodiversity and help reintroduce endangered species into the wilderness. They are there for our amusement.

• • •

I will never forget Lolita.

A female member of the L25 subpod, this young orca was removed from her natal L Pod, the largest of the three southern resident pods, during a controversial live-capture operation in Penn Cove, off Washington State, in which several other orcas died in the process back in 1970. Lolita was the only individual to survive these gruesome removals.

Now at fifty-six years of age, she has spent five decades a captive in the Miami Seaquarium Entertainment Park. A male orca named Hugo was her cage-mate for a while, but he died in 1980, likely from relentlessly smashing his rostrum against the walls of the can-sized tank. Since then, Lolita has been without the company of any of her species.

When Lolita turned fifty-one a few years ago, I was asked, along with two other marine mammal experts, to visit the Miami Seaquarium. The purpose was to observe her behavior and later testify about her physical and mental condition to support a legal action to secure her possible gradual reintroduction into her native habitat. In the protected waters of Puget Sound, at that time deemed a potential sea sanctuary, and still under human care, she would have finally been reunited with some of her family members.

The Seaquarium administration imposed a series of extremely specific restrictions on our work and was visibly—and audibly—displeased with having three conservationists nosing around their backyard. We got a room in a nearby motel and readied ourselves to observe Lolita and then draw our conclusions.

Staying in her company ended up being one of the most heartbreaking experiences of my life. I was stunned by how this orca—one of the most social mammals on Earth—had been able to survive for so long in such awful settings. In poor physical conditions, enclosed in a concrete tank she could hardly swim in and lacking any kind of environmental enrichment or protection from the sun, Lolita spent her days, months, and years alone—if one doesn't count a pair of Pacific white-sided dolphins she clearly didn't get along with. With Lolita, I was a witness to animal resilience in the face of our hominid arrogance.

From a bench in the oceanarium, I would see her stock-still, against the wall or on the bottom of the pool, just twenty feet deep at its center—the same length of Lolita herself. The rest of this bathtub was only twelve feet deep. An abysmal environment for a mammal that can swim up to one hundred miles per day, dive down to one thousand feet in the open ocean, and live in a tight-knit pod of relationships.

I watched Lolita dragging her flukes on the bottom and repeating the same behaviors, over, and over, and over again. And almost every day, with her dorsal fin collapsed, she performed on command like a submissive soldier, with nothing in her trained routine reminiscent of her life in the wild. Her entrapment brought me to tears.

Why didn't the crowd applauding from the benches surrounding the arena see what I saw? A profoundly scarred being, not only on the surface of her dark body but in her mind as well. Is it a lack of knowledge about this species, as it was for the demonized coyotes of my neighborhood? Is it convenience? Probably both. It's easy for us to enjoy a steak without thinking that the juicy piece of meat was once a living cow, a highly sentient individual with a distinct personality. For many of us, pigs, chickens, cows are commodities. And so is Lolita, even if she didn't wind up on a dinner plate.

Only once was I allowed by the Aquarium staff to move close enough to Lolita to almost touch her. As I approached and looked into her eyes, she gazed straight into mine, and I will never forget the pervading feeling of hopelessness that overwhelmed me. And when the judge in Florida ruled against the release of Lolita a year later, despite all our attempts to free her, the only thing I could think about was her pleading eyes. Disheartened.

The brain of Lolita, like mine, is wired to feel a broad spectrum of emotions including joy, desire, frustration, anger; and pain. But there were no traces of bliss or any other positive emotion in her. She was a sort of automaton. Captivity made her into something so different from her family members back in Puget Sound, who were able to express their whole range of feelings in their natural habitat.

Today, while reading an article about Lolita alone and at home, I feel close to her once again. I sense her solitude. I understand what it means to be separated from loved ones as I never did before.*

Spending time in the company of wild dolphins has always made the best case for them as emotional and empathetic beings with distinct personalities. I have witnessed firsthand the compassion of a dolphin mother while caring for her calf, of an individual helping a companion in distress. And once, while doing research in the unspoiled natural reserve of Rio Largartos in Yucatán, back in my early twenties, I saw a dolphin bereaved for the death of another.

Not far from shore, a female bottlenose dolphin acted grief-stricken for the death of what looked like her offspring. She was barely moving, keeping close to the still corpse of the young one. A couple of times, in the course of several hours, other individuals came by, almost as if they were asking this mother to rejoin the group and leave. But she didn't. The ocean conditions were rough and I couldn't go out on the water for more than a week after that day. When I finally returned to the same place, there was no trace of the mother or her dead calf.

* In 2022, The Miami Seaquarium, under new ownership, announced that Lolita has been retired from performing. Undoubtedly, it's a step in the right direction. It might be already too late for Lolita to be in the wild and with her own species, but continuing to push for her release in a sanctuary is still worth a try as her last chance for freedom.

In the Gulf of Corinth, Greece, a bereaved dolphin was observed remaining close to the floating, lifeless body of her newborn for several days, relentlessly trying to lift her offspring toward the surface to inhale with repetitive movements. She often touched the corpse with her flippers and rostrum in what appeared the last hope to revive and breathe new life into the body. And she didn't abandon her calf, not even to replenish herself with food. Her devotion seemed selfless. Untiring.

Like us, and several other terrestrial animals, cetaceans can experience grief, even if there are still questions about *how* they do it. Bottlenose dolphins may stay motionless and lose interest in eating, playing, and having sex. They may seek solitude, withdrawing from their companions to stay close to their lost one. Like us, dolphins experience both bright and dark emotions. And like most of us, and some other nonhuman species, with time passing, they realize life must go on, and eventually resume the natural rhythms of their existence.

Grief, after all, is part of being in this world.

• • •

It's true that, like intelligence, conscious emotion in Lolita and other ocean and land dwellers is challenging to comprehend, define, and measure. For comparison, I reflect upon how difficult it is for any of us to know what we are thinking or feeling at any given moment. Because we haven't categorized what these animals are feeling, though, doesn't mean that dolphins are not capable of emotions and vivid experiences. Seeing cetaceans in their natural environment, it's undeniable that these creatures have deep and rich emotional lives. And there is no doubt it's only by *getting to know* other animals better by observing them up close that we may stop viewing them as "things." The mystery now is not whether other nonhuman beings are conscious, but which are *not*.

If we can genuinely begin to grasp other creatures' intrinsic value in nature, consider their interests, even feel their pain, then, and only then, can we develop the empathy required to respect them as fellow beings.

Out in the wild, even a child will better discern who dolphins are and how they act in the company of their own "families." At sea, one will realize why we need to protect not just them but also the environment in which they live. These are some critical lessons in conservation to teach to a young mind.

Of course, not everyone lives close to the ocean and has the chance—or means—to be with free-ranging dolphins. I didn't grow up near the sea, nor I did have money to travel at a young age. For me, it was working two jobs—as freelance journalist and biologist for an Italian environmental nonprofit—that, early on, let me partake firsthand in whatever seasalty opportunities I could grasp.

Dolphins are *who*, not *what*, and they deserve rights. We should use our judgment and empathy toward these and other fellow animals and stop keeping them as prisoners for our entertainment.

Now that pandemic-induced confinement has given us all a taste of the mental and emotional stress that isolation can bring, perhaps we may better understand how caged creatures might feel.

9

A BIRD'S AWAKENING CALL

I sit outside in the garden. It's one of those days when I don't feel my usual self. To be honest, it doesn't happen often; I am an optimist, hopeful at heart.

At times, though, life hits with a rogue wave of melancholy; it's a wave that seems to come from nowhere, but when it crashes over you, you feel like you can't breathe.

Perhaps it's this pandemic dragging on. I ruminate on the questions that millions of us are undoubtedly asking at this precise moment. How long will the virus last? Will we ever go back to a normal life?

Or maybe what is weighing on my heart today is my dad's voice on the phone this morning, saying, with a hint of sadness, "We love you, we miss you so much."

I must head out. Outside, there is air; there are the sky and sun; there is the wind, a few scattered clouds, plants and animals. Outside is where nature is.

• • •

Now that the wasp colony has moved on and I've reclaimed my lounge chair, I lie on it, and observe my earth-friendly garden of native cacti, succulents, lupines, aromatics, and more. I am a proud mother. My offspring have grown well since I planted them a few months ago.

The evergreen *Aeonium* is in bloom. It's summer, an odd season for it to flourish in. But these are strange times we live in. Its oval, perky, yellow-painted inflorescences, evocative of lemon ice cream swirls, call for pollinators. And the bees respond. I haven't seen a bee for a while, and I am pleased these social and cooperative insects are back.

Then, I look up at the dark branches of the trees contrasting against the intense blue slice of the atmosphere. I inhale and exhale deeply, letting my mind rewind and pushing away the sense of sadness that has wrapped me tightly. Except, it's a strain for me to relax during the day. My brain is not wired to repose peacefully without doing something.

Being restless has its roots in my childhood. I was imprinted with the idea that leisure time is wasted time. "Unproductive time is something you can't get back in life," was my father's favorite reprimand. If my brother and I slept in more than the sanctioned eight hours per night, Dad would start stomping around the house like a marching soldier, making all kinds of noise to signify his disapproval. Perhaps the reason the walls of all the apartments and houses we lived in were filled with paintings was because of Dad hammering nails early in the morning.

Even now, many decades later, I still feel like my dad's admonition is haunting me. I do sleep late if I want to, and I don't have anyone telling me what to do, but there is always that faint whisper in my ear telling me that I could be doing something more meaningful and constructive with those hours thrown away in bed.

· · ·

Page 56 of *Becoming Wild* is waiting for me. Yesterday, I was so excited about getting a copy of Carl Safina's new book that I dove right into it, reading late into the night. I loved it. But this morning, I am not in the mood to focus on written words; at least, not yet.

I take a few deep breaths, this time to smell the sweet scent of the bright and fragrant flowers of my neighbor's winter jasmine. Then, I shut my eyes and make another attempt to unwind.

The warm desert air of the Santa Ana wind drives the relentless cacophony of cars and planes away, and there is a silence that's unusual for the City of Angels. Even the gardeners seem to have neglected to turn on their leaf blowers. Today, I can hear the foliage and twigs dancing free and birds chirping, and I begin to relax.

My thoughts are swirling and I feel as though I am floating in air or water, cuddled by unseen waves. I am finally at ease in the total tranquility of the moment.

• • •

Conk-la-ree!!!

All of a sudden, an intense warbling sound awakens my senses and brings my mind back from the apparent ocean of emptiness to the shore of my backyard.

Conk-la-ree, conk-la-ree!

I open my eyes and look around to see where the noise is coming from.

Conk-la-ree!!!

I turn 180 degrees and glimpse a red-winged blackbird perched on a branch of my overgrown tangerine tree.

I have spotted this species near the Ballona Freshwater Marsh down the hill from my house before, but I have never met one in my yard. This is a male leaning forward on the highest arm of my tree, singing its nasal song and puffing out his ruddy epaulets with a flamboyant air.

Is this some kind of a sign? I don't much believe in animal symbolism; however, I remember reading that seeing a red-winged blackbird is a positive omen. This songbird is letting me know the forces of nature are at work.

I am not sure if the wild is playing a game with my mind or what, but my senses are now awake, ready to absorb whatever the surrounding urban bestiary offers.

My jet-black, shoulder-padded visitor shouts another distinctive *Conk-la-ree*. I admire his stunning appearance, different from that of his female counterpart, which is usually adorned with a more subdued, streaky-brown uniform so as to better camouflage her body at the nest, typically hidden in dense shrubbery near marshlands.

As I watch and listen, I do wonder why his musical trill is so ostentatious in contrast to the other bird sounds I barely perceive in the background. It's almost as if this feathered fellow's high-pitched call, heard by his kind from afar, strains to overcome the typical urban roar of the city, even if today the wind has brushed some of the noise away.

The *Conk-la-ree* of my red-winged visitor could be the same sound that inspired French composer (and ornithologist) Olivier Messiaen to write *La Merle noir*, an impressive chamber work for flute and piano. The real-life song of a nightingale impassioned Respighi to write *Gli uccelli*. And Vaughan Williams's *The Lark Ascending*, a pastoral romance for violin and orchestra, was sparked by the seraphic song of that little brown bird on high. So many composers—Vivaldi, Beethoven, Handel, among others—have been captivated by birdsongs, interweaving the voices of goldfinches, doves, hens, and cuckoos into their timeless music.

Nature fills not just our eyes but our ears and soul, and the human heart longs to embrace it all.

Biological diversity can evoke joy, working as a sort of antidote for despair in us humans. The healing power of nature, even the faux wild of a city park or a backyard, is more recognized with every passing day. Still, I was surprised to read in a recent peer-reviewed scientific paper, filled with all sorts of statistics, that birds can make us happy! It seems that high bird diversity in the surrounding environment of a person's daily life may provide as much pleasure as "extra money in the bank." Even so, we are witnessing habitat degradation and loss, and because of it, an unprecedented decline of avian fauna.

I don't need to go far to see it.

Many years before the Playa Vista development was Playa Vista, an unspoiled wetland rich in endemic species once thrived. Red-winged blackbirds perched on the rushes and flew over the salt slough in great flocks just down the hill from my home, heading west to the ocean. It was christened Ballona. Some believe that, a long time ago, this inner bay welcomed gray whales during their migration, and the name might have been a misspelling of the Spanish *ballena*, meaning whale. Over the past couple of centuries, however, this primeval natural enclave for a large diversity of animals and plants has been gradually devoured by urban sprawl.

Elements of the original wetlands were still there when I moved to LA in the midnineties. Back then, Ballona was a tad reminiscent of what it once was. Countless birds migrating along the Pacific Flyway, from the far southern tip of South America to northern Alaska, would shelter in these brackish, freshwater marshes that offered food and refuge where they could recharge from their long, arduous journeys.

In an attempt to save the remnants of the original marshes, Charlie and I joined The Ballona Wetlands Coalition, a grassroots movement formed to prevent further damage to this residual habitat. We were enviro-naive back then. Still, we should have known it was a losing battle. Even after Steven Spielberg back-peddled from building his Dream-Works Studios there, the location of which was opposed by hordes of "tree-huggers" like us, there was no hope. But the coalition of animal-rights activists, advocates for red foxes, lovers of endangered least tern and Belding's savannah sparrows, protectors of riparian corridors, did not remain silent. We protested, led tours of the shrinking wetlands, and hosted restoration events in the sand dunes; we had no chance, though, against the unstoppable machine of greed.

"We saved it!" blazed on oversized signs along the roadsides of Playa Vista. But we did not. Little now remains of that ancestral wilderness, and what little was saved is just a shadow of what this place was. A mere appearance.

Recently, I took Genghis down the hill to the entrance to what endures of Ballona Wetlands. Hiding behind overgrown, smog-covered shrubs garbed with plastic bags waving like ghosts in the breeze, intersected by three-lane roads, traffic lights, electric poles, and endless rows of dilapidated RVs belonging to LA's growing homeless populace, there it was: *The Reserve*. Yes, there were the manicured pedestrian trails, quaint wooden bridges, strategically placed scenic outlooks with flamboyant educational signs, the man-made meandering streams, and some leftover puddles of marshland. But I couldn't shake off the contrived, Disneyland-esque feeling that this fragmented habitat now conveyed. A park for people to admire, but not a home for animals to flourish in.

Genghis on leash, I listened carefully for the tell-tale sounds of coots, flycatchers, herons, and geese. I should have been pleased to find a little biodiversity so near to home. Yet, this artificial lot of surviving nature provoked more grief for what was lost than pleasure for what had remained.

• • •

My little shoulder-padded visitor has now left the upper branch of my tangerine tree and I watch as he flies away and disappears in the distance. Even while we humans persist in putting our own ideas of development over the welfare of every other remaining living creature, a red-winged blackbird still rendered the gift of his song to the world, and I was an unintended, grateful recipient.

His loud voice is gone, but he has left the auditorium open for other sounds to come to life in my garden; sounds I haven't really noticed before today, not until I finally unlocked my mind to grant them access.

I hear the harmonious and gentle whistle, followed by *chip* notes, of the Anna's hummingbird. And as I turn to locate the origin of this melody, I can't miss this male, with its fiery iridescent chameleonic magenta tones, wings slightly sagged, perched on one of the drooping electric wires.

I don't even need to go outside to watch hummingbirds; over our morning coffee, Charlie and I spot them almost daily outside our living room window.

Only once have I seen a male Anna's perform his stunning

courtship display: flying high into the sky and then lunging abruptly, swooping to the ground in front of his potential partner and making a showy explosive popping sound at the bottom of the dive. A perfect Cirque Du Soleil performance by a feathered critter the size of a ping-pong ball and the weight of a nickel.

My inquisitive ear is now tuned in to other melodies. Is there a mourning dove around with her soothing *coo-coo* call? Can I distinguish the cheery-voiced house finch or the soft chirping of a warbler?

• • •

Bouncing back in time, I see my younger self tagging migratory pigeons in Sardinia and hiking, binoculars ready, along the smooth hills of Tuscany to identify bird species; I feel the cold morning breeze while waiting to record the sand martins emerging from their nests along the riverbanks in Emilia Romagna, or standing still while griffon vultures drifted around and around on the thermals above the rugged mountain peaks of the Monfragüe National Park of Extremadura in Spain. And I remember how I used to recognize so many different bird sounds, from raptors to cuckoos, from owls to sparrows, nutcrackers, and swifts.

Manuel, an ornithologist friend I met during my years

at the university back in Italy, taught me how to eavesdrop on birds and the surrounding wild. Of short stature, with dark, long hair and backpack bonded to his muscular shoulders, he could recognize and echo hundreds of nature-made sounds, then spell out the common and Latin names of countless species.

"*Ascolta* Madda, listen," Manuel would say, poking his head out the window of his Volkswagen van, "can you hear that short chirp? That's the sound of a great spotted woodpecker!"

Easy for you, maybe! I thought to myself, my ears and mind yet untrained in the sounds of wilderness.

His old mud-caked camper, smelling of patchouli oil, served as our field base. There, we ate, slept, and talked. Mostly about animals. Our feet did the rest, taking us where nature was still wild. From Manuel, I learned to listen, to see the unseeable.

• • •

This morning, as happened in my youth, the sound of songbirds brings me a sense of calm. The wave of melancholy is gone, replaced by a novel feeling of serenity.

I open my eyes. I am back in my yard, in the melodious natural microcosm of wild creatures I hear but not always see. Being trained to observe wildlife, I sometimes forget to listen to it.

Now, I am eavesdropping.

A few bird conversations are taking place. They are beyond my recognition. Still, a few sounds are vaguely familiar, perhaps faraway memories of my youth in the woods pushing to resurface. I can see, smell, and hear nature. And I am part of the physical world around me.

A *humming* noise makes me turn toward the blooming *Aeonium*, and I spot a Rufous hummingbird flying in front of one of the flowers. The bees are gone, and it's another species' turn to forage. I love the harmonic, recurring *hum* coming not from the syrinx of this little bird but from the aerodynamic forces produced as its tiny wings move, paired with the speed and direction of the wing movements. The Rufous is there for thirty, maybe forty seconds, and then it's gone.

I lost myself this morning. A blackbird visiting the tangerine tree found me, brought me back, and soothed my despair, filling my soul with harmonious sounds and pleasant memories. He reminded me that I am never alone when life is flourishing nearby and guided me to reconnect with nature through a newly attuned sense, one I had neglected for too long.

10

OPUS THE OPOSSUM

Opus is an adult male opossum, about the size of a fat domestic cat.

Opus has a pink nose, beady jet-black eyes, and mousy, rounded ears.

Opus's bristly hair is unusually long even for his hefty figure.

I am unsure where exactly Opus lives but I suspect it might be under my house.

And because of Opus, my vegetable garden has ceased to exist. I recently replaced a graveyard of unripe crop, crushed by his heavy feet before it could reach my kitchen, with more opossum-impervious greenery.

• • •

Since Opus is a nocturnal fellow, I only see him at night. My nose is not as keen at detecting his presence as Genghis, who lets me know in no uncertain terms that his number-one antagonist is strolling around in the backyard again. My pooch sprints like a rocket from his bed, and clumsy as usual, runs through the house cutting corners wherever he sees fit to reach the large double window facing our garden—sometimes neglecting the glass that separates indoors from outdoors. My dog doesn't deviate if Charlie or I happen to be inauspiciously in his path; he drives straight "through" us as if we were invisible. Tea stains on the ceiling of my living room are testimony to the day that Genghis, on his way to get to Opus, tossed me, and a full chai latte, in the air.

• • •

Genghis is perhaps even more obsessed with Opus than he is with squirrels. But Opus doesn't care about my large and gawky dog.

He did at the beginning. There was a time when Opus used to hiss, baring his needle-sharp teeth, and growl deeply, raising his pitch as Genghis profusely foamed at the mouth and barked like a rabid mongrel from behind the glass. Opus, though, quickly realized his bluster was needless, seeing that my canine companion was forbidden to go out at night.

So, when the sun sinks on the horizon, the backyard becomes Opus's space. Even the usual raccoons and skunks don't dare to enter.

Yes, there is an instant when this intruder glances at my furious mutt. Opus's pitch-dark eyeballs point at the hazy figure of Genghis, standing on two legs, with his wet nose mashed against the glass. But then, with nonchalance and an illusory middle finger, Opus turns his narrow snout around and with an involuntary grin, resumes his nocturnal habits.

Slow and stocky, methodic and hassle-free, Opus prowls the shrubs, rocks, and succulents, picking up whatever the evening menu offers. On occasion, I see only his long, rat-looking, scaly prehensile tail sticking out from behind one of my cacti.

On a couple of occasions, I spotted his tail wrapped tightly around a branch of the Chinese Strawberry Tree, body hung upside down for a moment, with his hind and front feet firmly grasping a couple of thinner branches. It was then that I noticed the striking similarity of Opus's hands to my own; the opposable large toes of his hind feet so closely resembling my thumbs.

His tapered tail, which bears only a few scattered hairs, is a remarkable tool that helps Opus while climbing and stabilizing his body. He can easily ascend and descend a tree the same way a telephone lineman uses his safety device when climbing to repair a cable on an electric pole.

And that's not all. The tail is something more; it's a fifth "hand" opossums use for other tasks, such as carrying small bundles of dead leaves and grass to line their sleeping dens with.

• • •

Behaving like an upside-down monkey is something I seldom see Opus do, but I love that he feels unhindered enough to act as he pleases in my presence. It allows me to observe his antics, to discover various nuances of his night-to-night behavior under the dim artificial lights of my house or the shine of a full moon.

I see this omnivorous creature gnawing on anything he can put his little, widely spread fingers on. And while probing, Opus drools noticeably. Not very gentlemanly on his part to drip like a mastiff; then again, the saliva is there to keep his mouth clean.

His extra-long whiskers, the vibrissae, are constantly at work; each of them lively with independent movements and able to transmit the sensory input they acquire from the surrounding environment. Despite his bulging eyes, Opus—like all his kind—has poor visual acuity and distant vision, but anything slightly touching those delicate vibrissae can set off a swift defensive response.

Nose to the ground, Opus is on the go. Earthworms seem to be the main dish tonight and my yard has many to offer, particularly this evening after a couple of rainy days. It's fascinating to discover how he eagerly explores different routes in the yard to rummage for food. Plants, worms, beetles, moths, and fallen fruit are among his favorites; Opus is far from being a finicky eater. And if one night I happen to miss watching his foraging activities in person, I always spot the remnants of his messy meals in the morning.

Cleaning up after an opossum is something I never in my life imagined doing.

• • •

Contrary to dolphins, opossums have one of the smallest brain-to-body-size ratios among mammals. This, bundled with the fact they rarely react when handled by humans due to their shy manners and lack of aggressive defense mechanisms, brands them as stupid creatures. But they are not; contrarily, they tend to excel at resolving tasks, at least those that we have been able to observe. As an example, opossums can outsmart dogs and cats in remembering where food is hidden in complicated mazes;

and they can quickly grasp how to distinguish between toxic and edible mushrooms, even when nearly identical in appearance.

Not so long ago, we thought we were the only bright organism on the planet. Now, we know it not to be true, and we recognize that our idea of a conscious brain needs revision. The more we learn about our fellow animals, including species not as charismatic as dolphins and great apes, the more we see their aptitude, even their cognitive abilities. That's one of the many reasons, at least for me, it's so fascinating to probe into the nocturnal, still undisclosed life of Opus and his kind.

• • •

The Virginia opossum is the only North American marsupial (pouched mammal); it's also one of the most misunderstood mammals native to this country.

Misconception, fueled by ignorance, probably comes from their bizarre giant-rat-like appearance, with large mouths that, when startled, open widely to display fifty sharp and intimidating teeth. Not many people realize it's all a bluff; opossums have a gentle demeanor and they are not malign or threatening in any way. But it doesn't matter; we humans still see these city dwellers as repulsive and antagonistic vermin to run from. So, they become shadows of the night, fleeting glimpses in a backyard or on the side of a street. And because they are not acutely streetwise, we often spot them as road pizzas, flattened and dead on our thoroughfares.

I feel privileged to be able to closely examine this mis-judged and solitary species in my green patch, and fortunate that Opus has chosen my garden as his home.

Pre-Opus, the last time one of these marsupials ended up in my backyard was over a year ago. And it turned out to be a surprising visit. . . .

• • •

I remember Genghis engrossed in his usual brawl with the eastern fox squirrels.

All of a sudden, I notice him running toward something slothfully moving on the grass, and the next thing I see is a hairy mouse-looking figure being violently shaken in my dog's mouth.

"Stop!" I scream to Genghis who promptly drops his catch, startled by the yell.

A small mammal lays on the ground. Stock-still. I move closer and recognize an orphaned young opossum, in broad daylight.

Genghis is back on the attack; he pushes the lifeless body around with his paws and nose, now unresponsive to my shouting to halt.

I am finally able to pull my large hound away from the little corpse and back into the house, but I can still feel Genghis's disapproving eyes following me from behind the glass.

The little opossum is supine, on its side and motionless, the body curved with a ventral flexion and with the disproportionally long tail coiled up like a miniature boa. Its mouth is wide open with bared teeth and a small stream of foaming saliva; the lips are drawn back and the pink tongue hangs out, touching the ground. The tiny, black button eyes are almost shut and its paws are locked in baby-looking fists. I smell an intense foul odor secreting from the anal glands.

• • •

I am aware that opossums "play possum." Deprived of specialized mechanisms of defense or attack and unable to outrun most enemies leaves them only with the lame intimidation display of crouching down and showing sharp canine teeth or, when facing an extreme threat, feigning death. This is a passive tactic to deter an aggressor, and not something unique to this species in the animal world.

I know opossums are tough creatures that can survive extensive violence, and this stress-induced catatonic state can last up to several hours. Lastly, I remember that young opossums are masters at playing dead.

But how could this little, delicate being have survived the forceful abuse of my bulky canine?

Still, I go back inside and hide behind the window's curtains, waiting for the little opossum to stop playing possum, to feel finally safe and leave. Minutes become hours. Many hours.

I call my husband.

"Charlie, I think the baby opossum is dead! Our beast killed it!"

Now, both of us are watching from behind the curtains. After all this time and after all the ill treatment, we cannot believe it might still be alive. We take a shovel from the garage and head out to pick up his lifeless little body.

As we are almost ready to open the back double window, the baby opossum slightly twitches his leathery ear, raises its head, looks around, and slowly wobbles toward the closest hiding spot like a drunk leaving the counter at a bar.

"Yeahhhhh!" I shout, unable to contain my exuberance.

The impulse is strong to grab this orphan and put him in a warm sock that might remind him of the maternal pouch it was born in; it's hard to fight the urge to save this lonely being. It wasn't long ago that this still-naked, blind, deaf, and tinier-than-a-jelly-bean joey made its tough journey to reach its mother's pouch. Single-handedly, it climbed from the opening of the birth canal to the pouch using its well-developed forelimbs and clawed digits. And even after reaching the pouch, its struggle wasn't over. Once in, scrambling in a forest of coarse and curly hair, it needed to quickly latch onto one of its mom's nipples. Failing to do so meant certain death. There are only thirteen teats in the pouch, and not all may be functional; if more joeys are born than the number of functional teats, as usually happens, the extra infants perish.

As a naturalist, I believe in leaving individual wild animals alone. Unless they unequivocally need us, they must make their own way in the world. Even in an urban world like mine.

The little opossum is behind a shrub and I say goodbye; at least for now.

Once again, I marvel at the magnificence of nature, at the beauty of every single creature.

• • •

Opus trots on the plantar surface of his naked feet, rocking his body like a rolling boat in rough waters. His thick and oily undercoat of white hair, which darkens toward the ends, keeps him warm and dry, especially tonight when the soil is moist and the temperature is oddly low for Los Angeles. His tail is trailing behind, slightly elevated, so there is no drag against the ground.

It's a full moon. I turn off the light and calm my dog with a bacon-flavored Nylabone so I can watch Opus without a hint of disturbance.

Opus stops near a pile of rocks I collected during the remaking of the backyard. He peers around and then starts grooming. This is something opossums do regularly, even if they always look like they've had a bad hair day.

Sitting on his hind legs like a tiny human and using his multifunctional tail as support, Opus licks his forefeet first; then, as cats do, uses his forepaws to carefully wipe his entire snout.

Opus is way better than I am at washing my hands and face; and self-care in general. Over and over, he cleans his face meticulously, his little hands drawing circular patterns to cover all parts. Then, the grooming shifts to his body fur to remove potential parasites; this time, he employs one of his hind feet as a comb.

Grooming the body is a long and scrupulous process for Opus; there is no hurry because being spotless can make the difference between life and death. Occasionally, the combing can also bring some extra nutriment for Opus—and perhaps fewer ticks for my dog, considering that opossums can consume thousands of these potentially disease-spreading arachnids in a single season.

Opus not only saves us from annoying ticks; he has the superpower of being immune to rabies and the venom of rattlesnakes and cottonmouths. He is truly a badass!

• • •

I know Opus won't be in my garden much longer. He's a nomadic creature and when all the available dinners in my yard are eaten, Opus will vanish. I am also aware he won't live long. Two, maybe three years, at most. That's the lifespan of these marsupials, one of the shortest on Earth for its size. An existence that can be even further curtailed by a car accident, malnutrition, or parasitic infections, these being the main causes of death for this wondrous urban dweller.

But for now, Opus is here. Tomorrow, I can't say. Surely, I will miss him when he's gone.

11

SQUIRREL WARS

I am in the backyard with an old copy of *Catch-22*.

I feel relaxed and ready to dive into Joseph Heller's iconic novel when a high-pitched squeal almost ruptures my eardrums. I spin around to see my one-hundred-pound dog hanging from our Chinese strawberry tree.

One of his front legs is trapped in the Y of two branches, and his body is hanging a foot above ground like a quartered cow in a slaughterhouse; except his head is up, not down.

"*Aaaaahhhhhhoooooooo,*" Genghis screams with an almost-human sound.

I throw *Catch-22* on the floor and run toward him. He's

howling and his entire body is shaking in fear as I use all the strength I can muster to lift his dead weight; but I fail.

Genghis lets loose with another ear-piercing "Aaaaahhhhhhooooooo," this time just inches from my face as, once again, I strain to disengage him from the branches. Somehow, I manage to lift him enough to free his leg.

My mutt is back safe on the ground, quivering but now licking every bare part of my body.

"It's okay," I assure him as I massage his leg, moving it back and forth to see if he has broken anything. "It's okay, pup, it's okay," I repeat to him over and over while he is still in full vibration mode.

His oversized tongue leaves damp streaks on my face. When it comes to being inspected for any physical injury, my dog trusts me unconditionally.

Nothing seems broken, and Genghis limps a few steps backward, keeping his eye on me to ensure I am not deserting him. Abruptly, we both hear a rapid sequence of rattling chirps; we look up at the highest branches of the strawberry tree, and there's the culprit, staring down at us mockingly.

Now, I understand why Genghis got stuck up the tree in the first place. There was a squirrel to catch!

· · ·

The war started when Genghis walked into his new backyard as a three-month-old pup. Since then, the squirrels residing in the large trees of our garden have been his daily fixation. With their bushy tails and large eyes, these rodents occupy almost the entirety of my dog's garden time.

With all the hours Genghis has spent observing them, turning his large head up and down and right to left, he could be one of the greatest squirrel experts in the world. He knows about their daily movements and some of their hiding spots for nuts, and he is probably aware that during the fall they bury more food than they eat. My dog is familiar with their unique vocal repertoire made up of screeches, rattles, barks, and snorts—their alarm calls—and the *kuk*, *muk-muk*, and *quaa* they use during mating.

The only thing my mutt doesn't know is how to actually catch one. Despite hundreds of hunting attempts, with much paw raising and pointing, he has always failed miserably, not so differently from when he tries to capture lizards. This last accident that left him hanging from the tree was probably Genghis's most humiliating moment in front of the squirrels.

But the ongoing war between my dog and the rodent squad dwelling in my garden is not the only one storming here in the City of Angels. . . .

• • •

An East versus West battle that began almost one hundred years ago still rages between two rival gangs of squirrels in some LA neighborhoods. Up and down branches and poles, along electric wires and hopping from one fence to the next, the SoCal's native western gray squirrel is battling to hold a leftover patch of ground against its imported adversary: the eastern fox squirrel. The latter, which hitched a ride to California at the start of the twentieth century as "domestic pets" in the belongings of residents of the National Soldiers' Home (now the West LA Veterans' Affairs campus), are survivors. And trouble makers.

While our salt-and-pepper-colored Cali squirrels eat and distribute mostly acorns, supplemented by tree nuts and seeds of pinecones, the frisky Easties are opportunistic and omnivorous. They munch on anything they can get their little paws on, usually favoring larger meals. For them, size matters. They seem to opt for edibles that minimize search time but not handling time. And they balance the spatial distribution of foodstuff with the safety of the area, predator risk, toxin avoidance, and nutritional value of their meal. Plenty of assessments to make for a little rodent.

These red-furred mammals are also true conquistadors that aggressively expand their territory. And if that isn't enough, they reproduce like rabbits! It's no wonder our indigenous fluffy-tailed and less hostile Grays have been outnumbered by their belligerent opponents, becoming almost a rare sight in Los Angeles environs.

• • •

For most Angelinos, this doesn't mean much. The arboreal squirrels have been part of the LA scenery for years, and people pass these taken-for-granted critters by, unaware that one species is replacing the other.

For me, though, it's different. When I moved from Italy to the West Coast and saw a squirrel eating nuts on a picnic table at the University of California for the first time, I was captivated by these animals.

In my country, squirrels are not as bold as the California types. I have seen both, the invasive gray, introduced from the eastern part of North America, and our native red squirrel scampering around while hiking in the Alps and Apennines of Italy. But I had never seen one perched next to a Diet Coke and a bag of Doritos, sharing lunch with a group of scholars. The students at my university seemed numb to the presence of these rodents scurrying around them; they barely noticed their presence, or avoided them as if they were king-sized rats. Contrarily, in my years at UCLA, I was so mesmerized by these critters and their antics I found it hard to study. I may never have gotten my Ph.D. reading outdoors there.

My problem is I often find animals more entertaining than people, and squirrels never fail to amuse me with their funny and charming demeanor.

• • •

Even if it has been mostly unnoticed, it *does* matter that the imported Easties are displacing the native Grays in Los Angeles. As often happens in nature, introduced species tend to skew the balance of things, affecting the ecosystem in which they move.

Every time we clear-cut timber, mine for minerals, or add a pipeline; every time we build roads, erect buildings, construct freeways, bridges, ports, and more, we destroy habitats occupied by an array of nonhuman organisms, and fragment what's left of their territories. With our actions, we change animal distribution, occurrence, and abundance. We alter the entire dynamics of day-to-day interactions between and within species. Who remains is frequently the toughest survivor, able to adapt to a brutal city existence. Some of these fighters we see; others—such as the coyotes in my neighborhood—we only hear. Rarely do we keep the well-being of other creatures in mind in our race to expansion.

Often, even smaller, more localized "improvements," such as the removal of trees and shrubs from a community like mine, can have adverse outcomes and threaten organisms.

These changes can favor invasive and more opportunistic species to colonize an area.

Western and eastern squirrels are an instance of animals competing on a fine scale in my neck of the woods. And the Easties—thanks to their generalist habits—are superior opponents of the more picky Grays in a fragmented, less-woodsy environment like Los Angeles, and thus the clear bread (or nut) winners.

It's not only LA that got the Easties: these tiny immigrants were dumped from here to other areas of Southern California lowlands, damaging fruit trees, and consequently, becoming nuisances. All of it, while their Gray counterparts were decreasing in number by the day. Too bad, considering that our native squirrels are not just great indicators of the well-being of natural conifer and oak habitats; they are also prodigious gardeners. They literally plant trees by hiding—and at times forgetting—their preferred nuts and acorns from our native forests. These mini-farmers are also large consumers of a particular fungus that, when dispersed through their scats, allows pine and oak tree roots to better absorb water.

• • •

Hiding acorns is something squirrels are masters of, and they usually do it as scatter-hoarders, proactively stashing for cold weather when food will be scarce. Not only can they conceal and bury up to ten thousand nuts per year over large distances, but they typically retrieve up to four thousand of them!

It's remarkable to watch squirrels trying to locate the nuts they have buried far and wide because it's not random at all; and I can spend hours observing them. Many species of squirrels artfully arrange and hide their stash according to the type of nut, a behavior known as *chunking*. This is something that later on will be useful to them in remembering where they have concealed their food. And they don't just access their stockpiled pantries with their sense of smell. Squirrels utilize their spatial memory to help them map out the surrounding territory to locate their meals. It's a little like us using landmarks to find a restaurant, a florist, or a movie theater.

But because a squirrel's world is rife with nut thieves, they've learned how to be sneaky and deceitful when it comes to defending their pantry. If other squirrels are around, an individual may pretend to bury a seed in a specific spot in front of a potential thief. When its fake burial performance is over, the shrewd squirrel quietly scurries off with the nut stashed in its mouth to a new secret hiding place while the unfortunate burglar goes after the empty hiding place, hoping for a free meal. Some less-sophisticated squirrels just steal the nuts from the paws of others bypassing any subterfuge, as I often witnessed from those inhabiting my garden.

• • •

In my yard, I have seen Easties conceal their edible trophies near my micro-oasis of succulents or in one of the several terracotta pots harboring the miniature herb garden. They hide their snacks between the thyme and basil, or next to the abundant plants in my mint collection: peppermint, spearmint, mojito, and chocolate. I watch their activities out of sheer curiosity. For me, nosiness is a good starting point for observation of animal behavior because it comes with no preconceived assumptions.

When looking at the imported Easties, my mind—fueled by conflicting emotions—must go an extra mile because, despite them being intriguing and charming, I am acutely aware they are not meant to be here in the first place.

If we take the time to be inquisitive, we can discover fascinating things around us we have never perceived before in our day-to-day lives. Now, I wonder how many of my neighbors have stopped to view where and how our little, hectic non-human friends conceal their meals in our backyards; how they cunningly burglarize each other; how they consume their food.

• • •

During my walks, I search for squirrel nests, called dreys. It's a treasure hunt. These creatures are shrewd in hiding their abodes in the upper branches of trees shielded by dense foliage—both to raise their young and to shelter from the elements. It's not easy to notice them, especially from a distance. So, instead of looking up, I stare down at the base of the trees that still endure along my streets, hunting for fresh remnants of squirrel meals. Half-eaten nuts, chewed-up pinecones that look like apple cores, discarded seeds. After locating these, I look up, almost sure to discover an occupied drey.

Once, I saw a female squirrel building her drey into a fork of one of the high limbs of a large oak tree down the street, almost flawlessly camouflaged into the thick leafage. With its roots and branches chopped off so as to not hinder the sidewalk or electric wires, this oak would not have been her ideal abode in a more natural setting. Around here, though, this tree was *la crème de la crème*.

Armed with binoculars, zooming in between leaves and branches, I spotted this Lilliputian builder loosely weaving together sticks and twigs of different lengths. Such a handy squirrel! The final outcome was a nest shaped like a large, messy spaghetti bowl with a comfy inner padding of leaves, shredded bark, and grass. It somehow reminded me of the coziness of my hammock, strung between coconut palms under the stars of the Biosphere Reserve of El Palmar in the Yucatán Peninsula of Mexico, back when I was studying sea turtles.

Since I first noticed my Lilliputian builder, I've gone back to the same spot often to visit her. As usual, patience is of the essence. Sometimes, I can neither see nor hear her. Other times her familiar *chuk chuk* noise reverberates somewhere above me. A few weeks ago, I only saw the end of her fluffy tail sticking out of the drey. It was a cold, dewy LA morning on which I, too, would have rather stayed curled up in my own drey instead of strolling outside with Genghis. But there have been many instances when I am able to trace her antics from branch to branch and tree to tree.

One day, though, while searching for my little squirrel with binoculars, I observe something entirely different in midair: a red-tailed hawk.

I often see these raptors while meandering on the dirt paths of the Playa Vista bluffs near my house. While Genghis runs madly up and down the hill, I watch them soar effortlessly in wide circles against an intense blue sky, riding thermal air currents, then swooping down to capture prey with their talons. I've noticed them patiently schooling their fledglings how to hunt and survive in the milieu of the Playa Vista suburbs. And I've spotted their nest, a hefty bowl of sticks lined with green, thinner branches, hidden in the crown of an old oak tree that stands lonesome at the topmost part of the slope.

Seldom do I see red-tailed hawks during my wanderings

around home. Perhaps it's because I don't often walk nose-up. I continually need to keep an eye on what my dog is up to, so that I don't wind up being pulled to the ground if he gets excited about a cat or a squirrel and takes off at *Bugatti*-speed. But that morning, this large bird of prey, with its broad, long, rounded wings, and trademark cinnamon-red tail was circling above the squirrel's drey in the *crème de la crème* oak tree.

I never saw my little squirrel there again. Maybe she moved to live in a denser forest of nut trees. That's what I love to think. Or maybe it's just *Nature, red in tooth and claw*.

• • •

Even if I take note of squirrels while walking with Genghis in the neighborhood, my backyard remains the paramount venue to view them. I always have a front-row seat reserved. At sunrise, I can watch the first grooming, which usually occurs before two or more individuals start performing circus acts, hopping from branch to branch and from cable to cable, chattering as they leap through the air. I hear them barking back at my dog. I see them holding pine cones in their tiny hands as if they were corn on the cob, or sitting on low branches with their tails curled over their backs for a well-earned, post-activity siesta. I once witnessed one of them deploying its tail almost like a parachute to land on a patch of grass after falling out of the Chinese strawberry tree.

My yard squirrels are mostly Easties. I rarely see a SoCal native.

Unfortunately for the poor, outnumbered Grays, being under siege from the opportunistic Easties is not their only problem. West Coasters have never been eager to move out of their accustomed home range that, in the last decades, has shrunk due to human development. What were once acrobatic jumps among trees and shrubs in the wilderness are now mostly hops on an obstacle course of concrete walls, roofs, and electric cables. And now, the holdout against the eastern fox squirrels is nearing the end as our native squirrels become more isolated to small pockets of turf, which leads to inbreeding and moves them a step closer to local eradication.

The western gray squirrels are not the only species in these environs to inbreed and face annihilation for lack of habitat connectivity. Not too far away from me, in the Santa Monica hills, mountain lions too are constrained to smaller and smaller areas because their habitat is hemmed in by urban growth, freeways, and the ocean. For these large cats, signs of inbreeding are severe enough they bear physical evidence: kinked tails, shaped like the letter L, have been observed in a handful of lions. For scientists, that's a sign individuals have started mating with close relatives.

Coyotes and eastern fox squirrels are the survivors here.

And if coyotes teach us a lesson of coexistence, observing animals acclimatized to us with an open mind can teach us much about resilience against all odds. Taking notice of these naturalized eastern fox squirrels led me to learning the full story of their species' impact in California, but the squirrel itself is following only its own nature and its will to endure our power of destruction.

• • •

On a large branch of the Chinese strawberry tree, an Easty emits a warning screeching sound and fluffs up its reddish banner-like tail to look bigger and display its dominance. My dog barks, and the white hair on his back stands up like he's an eighties punk rocker.

The war continues.

12

APOCALYPSE NOW

California is burning again; I can feel it down in my throat as I wake up.

I wash my face and wonder how some people can still deny the role of human-induced climate change when raging flames here have now scorched an area almost as big as Connecticut.

I think, well, what could get worse today? Out with my dog out for a mini-walk, I breathe some thick, ash-filled, unsafe air. The sky is smoky-gray and the sun seems a giant, hazy orange. And it's only 10:00 am. No garden meditation this morning.

Back in my home office, I catch up on more news before sinking into grant-writing mode to resuscitate my environmental nonprofit. It's too late before I realize that reading the paper is indeed a bad idea; today's news revealed that things actually *could* get worse, both on political and economic fronts.

I look out the window, and for the first time, I feel there is no place to go. Even the simple act of breathing is a problem.

• • •

To distract myself, I try to find refuge in my halcyon memories of the wild. I have so many recollections to pick from (one of the advantages of aging). It's like grabbing a stuffed animal out of one of those claw machines. Except I always win. If I can't be in nature, at least I can daydream a little and relieve my mind from dire images of flames, smoke, and devastation.

I am transported to the cold tip of Tierra del Fuego, in Patagonia. And there I am on the deck of a boat, bundled up like the Michelin Man. Around me, there is no haze nor smoky air, and I can almost feel the unpredictable, relentless wind of the Beagle Channel striking my face. The pungent odor of the cormorant guano fills my nostrils as the boat approaches Martillo Island. I hear the raucous noises of the Magellanic penguins. They wobble on the sun-bleached pebbles in their tuxedo vests, calling out to their life partners. As the mounting wind whips spray off the waves and wets my clothes, my hands grip firmly onto the railing and Charlie. For a moment, a pleasing sensation of freedom envelops me. Then, the horizon fades into a somber gray mist that swallows the entirety of the landscape. The icy, damp air is darkened by ash. All my senses still attempt to hold tight to this memory. But it's too late. I am back in LA, in the office, under the dim light of this doom-filled morning.

• • •

It's not just California scorching. It's the American West. And these unprecedented wildfires are far from normal. Climate change has amplified the occurrence of droughts, extremely hot days, and consequently, outbursts of inferno scenes.

A virus, sooner or later, will either go away or become endemic; not this. No jab can stop what we are doing to the only planet we have.

As a scientist, I realize that stopping this snowballing crisis must be at the top of my priorities because it is the most pressing threat we are facing today.

• • •

The tricky question is: What can I do about it?

Recently, I've found myself thinking a lot about this. Or at least, more than usual. Perhaps it's just being trapped inside. Maybe it's because apathy is rampant these days, an insidious emotion that can permeate our lives, producing anxiety, fatigue, anger, disappointment, and resentment. Apathy can also paralyze our senses and make us numb, disconnecting us from other human and nonhuman beings.

I believe apathy is something we must consciously fight with all our will. And nature is here to help, ready to throw us a line and teach us how to breathe again and rewire our minds. It's up to us to catch that line.

• • •

Observing wildlife has nurtured my appreciation and respect for other living organisms, and with respect comes the responsibility to act. Undoubtedly, I would have been quite content with passing my days observing the behavior of other creatures, without angst. Yet, as I got older, the wilderness around me started to change, and a little at a time, I changed with it.

Many of the natural places of my youth are almost gone now, and it saddens me. I am troubled by what's happening to our land and seas. I am worried about failing nature. I fear losing all those open spaces where I experienced such natural beauty as a young girl.

I have been immersed in learning the story of human impact on the oceans for my entire adult and professional life. Oceans have endured over their multibillion-year existence, yet our species is the most dangerous enemy they face. There is no place we can't reach; our footprints are everywhere. Even the high seas, belonging to no one and thus free to everyone, are not so far away that we cannot exploit them for profit. We scoop everything from the oceans, not just what sustains us. In doing so, we deplete marine habitats and life-supporting systems. Over ninety percent of large predatory fish are now gone, with sharks, bluefin tuna, and swordfish in dramatic free-fall; and we feed further and further down the food chain.

We treat the oceans as supermarkets with infinite shelves filled with goodies, then we turn around and use them as garbage dumps. Plastic has spread far and wide in the sea. I have seen stranded whales' stomachs filled with plastic bags, ropes, golf and tennis balls, spray canisters, surgical gloves, and sweat pants. And living creatures are only part of what we take. Our petroleum addiction has led us into deeper and deeper waters to the oil-rich seabed. But like fish, oil from the ocean floor is not an endless resource.

What if the hawksbill turtles I studied back in my twenties never return to the Mexican shores where they were hatched? If the Vaquita porpoise, endemic to the Sea of Cortez, in Mexico, and now the rarest marine mammal, disappears forever? Or if the remaining few hundred North Atlantic right whales—so-called because they were the right whale to hunt—are pushed to extinction due to ship collisions and entanglement in fishing gear? I am afraid all those wonderful memories I rescued from my brain-claw machine will be all that are left.

• • •

I am not alone in asking *What can I do?* Charlie and I spend hours reading and discussing conservation and political issues, and both of us try to do anything that might make even a crumb of a difference. My husband believes in being ruthlessly self-critical of one's actions, and if I am truthful with myself, I am still doing close to nothing to address this ecological meltdown. After all, I am the environmentalist with a carbon-zero garden who still flies back to Europe. I am a carbon sinner. Guilty as charged.

Most of my friends ask the same *What can I do?* question too, except for those who cannot bear to think about it because it's so overwhelming, and the mere mention of the topic upsets and depresses them. A newly coined word for how many people currently feel about climate change is *eco-anxiety*, defined as "the chronic fear of environmental doom." This modern phenom-enon creates a great sense of worry, inhibiting our ability to fight the ecological emergency we are witnessing.

There is nothing wrong with feeling worried. I do, for sure. Truly, though, I don't think hiding my head in the sand

and refusing to address the issue is a valid option. The reason for recognizing climate threats is not to define Armageddon but to prevent it. We often forget that saving the planet means saving ourselves. Earth will outlast us, in one form or another. Humans are bound to be transient, as all other species.

Yet, I continue to struggle.

• • •

To try as individuals to make a difference for Mother Earth, many of us recycle, ride bicycles, clean up a beach, plant a garden, avoid plastic, go vegan, click to support an online campaign, sign a petition, and vent on the social media channel of choice. And then life goes on. Of course, everything helps and individual behavior matters, but is this enough, especially when too many people continue to live as if everything is fine? No; this is not enough to bring about the *immediate* changes needed.

The main problem is that the ecological disaster we are seeing now in America—and worldwide—is not only overwhelming, but also more and more a political crisis of leadership.

Honestly, I have never paid too much attention to politics. I don't particularly relish politics. I grew up in Italy where the government has been corrupt for such a long time that any attempt at fixing it seemed irremediable to me. This is not an excuse for not being participatory in bringing the change that my country needed, and still needs, to get out of its gritty situation. Then again, I never thought Italy's actions or policies threatened anyone on a global scale as America's actions do.

Now, I've lived in the States for more than twenty-six years. Sadly, I can't afford the luxury of steering clear of politics anymore. The whale in the room in this country (and elsewhere) is a political system that favors economic gain over the well-being of the planet.

That's why, if I have to focus my efforts on what I can do to help nature, besides living a more sustainable life, I must act to make sure the political system works the way it should. This is where I believe I need to concentrate my energies in the immediate future, as a scientist, a conservationist, and a responsible, active member of our society.

• • •

In my job as the president of an environmental nonprofit, the *What can I do to save the planet?* question comes up often. Frequently tied to: *Is there still hope?*

"Yes, you *ought* to do something to avert this global crisis," I always say, to emphasize that individual action is essential, "and there is still hope."

But hope demands, or better yet, *is*, action and commitment. It's not hoping someone else will do something. Because climate change is here, knocking at everyone's door.

Exploring animal behavior can provide a greater understanding of both nonhuman beings and our wrong-doing toward them. By spending time observing the nature around us closely, we become better informed about nearby environmental issues. Curiosity can lead us to cultivate a better knowledge of those problems, and then the motivation to work hard to involve other people, therein building a sense of stewardship in the community. Finally, now fortified with a squad of allies, we can lobby for more accountable, greener leaders, and impact the political process.

Engagement in fixing one or more tangible issues with the help of others offers a productive relief from the anxious stagnation of these hazy times we live in, and assuages the feelings of despair and withdrawal that can frequently overwhelm us. Because, in the end, doing something meaningful also makes us feel good. And the better we feel, the more we want to do meaningful things and inspire others to do the same.

We need all levels of government to cooperate in taking courageous climate actions, and all levels of government need to listen to what we have to say. Volunteering and lobbying at the local level (pushing for policies that will cut our reliance on fossil fuels and such), participating in protests, and writing about issues that are important to the health of our planet are a few ways that work for me as a scientist and writer. But each and every one of us can find our own paths to effecting change based on our personal strengths. Only then can we raise our voices together.

• • •

When we don't work effectively as a collective, we risk losing everything.

Take the Ballona Wetlands Coalition, the grassroots movement formed to stop the Playa Vista development. In the midnineties, several organizations attempted a collaborative effort to save the leftover marshland, but there were disagreements among the groups about how to proceed. The arguments were seemingly endless. I remember Charlie and I going to meetings, asking, "Why don't we put aside our differences and focus on effecting *real* and *specific* change?" It didn't happen. Now, little is left of the marshes. I have seen this happen over and over again in different sectors of our work. While we tree-huggers fight among ourselves, the window of opportunity to alter our current path is closing swiftly.

I have also experienced firsthand the difference we can make when we *do* act together. For many years, my team and I have collected data on the coastal bottlenose dolphins off

Los Angeles. Because this population travels up and down the shoreline from Baja California, Mexico, to Oregon, I reached out to other researchers in an attempt at collaboration. I thought that sharing information would provide a better scenario of what's going on with the "metropolitan" bottlenose dolphins moving along this stretch of the Pacific. At the outset, I encountered stiff resistance. Everyone seemed to be madly proprietary and protective of their data. But then, with a lot of coaxing, one at a time, they all came around: scientists from different universities and NGOs, bridging the tip of sunny Baja to foggy Northern California. We teamed up. Shared numbers. Matched images of dorsal fins. Worked and published together. And by unifying our strengths and knowledge, we now understand far more about this dolphin population and its health status than we ever did before, which gives us a better picture of the overall condition of the marine ecosystem. It's through this shared information and combined expertise that we now have new tools, and a better chance, to protect the animals we have all dedicated decades to.

On an even smaller scale, I think about my neighborhood and the adjacent ones, and all the people who read Nextdoor. What a powerful tool to bond citizens Nextdoor could be! What a difference for our communities we could make if Nextdoorians could find common ground instead of being quarrelsome with each other, and tap into some of the enviro issues we are facing at our doorsteps. No more irate anticoyote mobs. Simply folks observing their surrounding world, learning from it, and strengthening their appreciation for the nearby nature, all necessary for effecting change. Individual actions *can* be part of collective action. We can start in our backyards, and then grow from there.

For me, something worthy came from the pandemic. The virus slowed me down and enabled me to see and appreciate the fauna swarming nearby. Paying careful attention to wildlife, even in a "micro" sense, helped me avert the stress and sorrow of this unfamiliar period. But again, being a scientist is not a prerequisite for perceiving the surrounding wilderness. I reflect on a twofold opportunity here, for Nextdoorians and others. By developing observational skills, anyone can find relief from uncertain times. And by actually viewing the neighboring biota, collecting and sharing data, anyone can also contribute to our collective knowledge. It's a win-win.

Engaging the public in hands-on conservation is something Charlie and I have been committed to since the nineties. It is also something very close to our hearts. A couple of years ago, at Ocean Conservation Society, we started the Be Balloon Aware campaign to raise awareness about plastic pollution and its direct effects on the ocean and marine mammals we study. When people release party balloons into the air, they eventually end up in our waters. They are among the top-ten types of debris found during coastal cleanups. Animals can become entangled in balloon strings, making them unable to fly, swim, feed, or effectively defend themselves from predators. Because this is an issue that crowds can easily see while strolling on the beach here in LA, we turned to citizen scientists for help. We organized volunteers up and down the California coast to gather balloons and data on this debris, and we now intend to affect some of the existing laws.

Conservation initiatives to fight climate change that engage a broad range of individuals in doing science are not hard to find. One example: GLOBE Observer, an international network of citizen scientists and researchers working together to learn more about our collective environment and shifting climate. From counting species in the ecosystem to monitoring pollutants in rivers, they enlist folks and communities in a wide range of science-related projects.

Opportunities are abundant.

• • •

I look out the window. It's still noon, but it seems like dusk. The sun is an orange dot. *It's Apocalypse Now!* But tomorrow is a new day that will hopefully bring new ideas and possibilities to make this world a little better.

13

LIZARD! LIZARD! LIZARD!

It's midwinter in LA. Fire season has passed, and these days it gets dark at 5:00 p.m. and is a tad chilly. But this morning is hot, like the weather is celebrating a new week in the City of Angels with an unusually sunshiny daybreak. So, I too commemorate the event by taking Genghis for a stroll along the bluffs overlooking this seemingly endless city, only a twenty-minute walk from my house.

My mutt is ecstatic; only saying the word "Dunb"—code for *Are you ready to go for a walk on the bluff near Dunburton street?*—puts Genghis in vibration mode. His body shakes excitedly and he pants vigorously, hovering around the front door, at the same time keeping an eye on where I am, just in case I get distracted.

• • •

It has been a while since we hiked these slopes of soft chaparral. The tall, green grass is gone but the all-pervading smell of sagebrush fills the lungs. This time of year, Santa Ana winds blow through the mountain passes, bringing warm and dry air from the desert, turning our skies to a crystalline cobalt blue. The iconic Hollywood sign on Mount Lee looks so close I can almost touch it.

Genghis is off the leash. I enjoy not constantly being my dog's master and giving him his deserved freedom. After all, it's a weekday and the upland trails are deserted.

Like that battery bunny with a full charge, he sprints up and down the knolls. At times, I see him loping his way downhill, with a jubilant, wide smile, his long tongue dangling back and forth.

He's at full speed and I already know what will happen next. I prep for impact; my legs bent like a sumo wrestler, arms fully extended with palms open toward him. I scream, "Stooooooooop!" But I know my oversized hound won't.

One would think he might miss me, swerving at the last minute without stopping. Wrong! Bursting with excitement, Genghis doesn't hit the brakes. Raising a cloud of dust, he slams into one of my bent legs, which slows him down a bit, then rockets, muzzle first, into the nearby brush. He emerges with fluid and relaxed tail wagging, coming back toward me for a few wet licks of elation.

Thirty minutes are plenty to run him out of steam. The sun is now high in the sky and my mutt trots next to me, back on the leash, ready for the second phase of his "Dunb" time: the lizard hunt.

Genghis's half-labrador side never really kicked in; instead of catching and retrieving tennis balls like my old lab Burbank, this canine is lizard obsessed. It doesn't matter if he's strolling on a leash along the sidewalk or trotting unrestricted on dirt trails.

As Genghis sniffs around for reptiles, his mighty nose is fully in action. He could find his way back home from here, if he wanted to, by relying on overlapping circles of familiar scents. Outside his immediate range, he might pick up the smell of a recognizable dog in the next circle. That smell might point to another circle that feels memorable for a particular tree, a trash can, a fence. And so on. It's a little like how cellular phone coverage relies on interconnected footprints from different cell towers.

When he is on the go, Genghis's favorite prey-of-the-day is the *Uta stansburiana elegans*, or common side-blotched lizard, named for the dark mark behind the armpit. His almost

childish enthusiasm for these saurians is reminiscent of someone I recognize well. . . . Me.

• • •

Since lizards are perfectly adapted to Italian city environs and
were readily accessible in my parents' backyard, they became
part of my urban bestiary when I was a child, and the focus of
my obsessive observations.

I can't recall all the hours spent probing into the lives of
the greenish *Podarcis sicula*, aka the Italian wall lizard, basking on
its flat belly on the concrete or hunting back and forth at the
edge of my mom's rose bushes in search of prey.

I learned the meaning of the word patience as I worked
out how to gather data and design an ethogram: an inventory of
behaviors displayed by individual animals.

Back then, I didn't know these naive field studies would
shape the rest of my life.

• • •

My reverie is broken by Genghis nearly pulling my arm out
of the socket. A group of yellow warblers sitting on the slim
branches of a coyote bush hastily take to the sky, scared by my
dog as I let go of the leash to avoid being dragged into the
shrubs.

The white tip of his tail wags wildly; if he could talk, I am sure he would be shouting, "Lizard! Lizard! Lizard!"

Over the years, Genghis has adopted a variety of methods to hunt these reptiles. If his enemy is sunning on a pile of rocks, he strikes a pointer pose with paw folded and suspended in the air, waiting for the perfect moment to attack. A nonchalant demeanor with abrupt leaps is an alternate form of pursuit when lizards are on the move. But nearly pulling my arm out of the socket while on the leash seems to be his favorite.

Whatever the technique of the day might be, Genghis has never caught a lizard in his life. Not only that; he usually ends up making a fool out of himself, the same way he does when chasing squirrels in the backyard. Sticking his nose straight into the spines of a saguaro cactus or falling into a storm drain and sliding fifty feet, face first, down the mossy ramp while hunting a southern alligator lizard are just two examples of his goofiness.

Missed attempts aside, Genghis and I enjoy playing citizen scientists with lizards in our not-so-wild community. So far, with the help of field guides, I have identified several different species while wandering in the neighborhood and on the bluffs. It still astounds me what one can discover with only a guide, open eyes, and a pair of sneakers!

Finding two of these natives, the southern alligator and

the western fence lizard, is easy. I don't even need to leave my backyard. These homeys hang around all day, sunlight permitting, and I often lay in the lounge chair and catalog their activities. Typically, they spend several minutes thermoregulating to warm their bodies on a sunlit spot of our Chinese strawberry tree; then, they do some ant and spider hunting among the strands of grass. After that, more sunbathing to raise the body temperature, and on to investigatory poking in and out crevices in the fence. Later, they take to some athletic climbing up the overgrown Indian laurel fig tree, with toes curling and uncurling to generate the suction pressure that enables this animal to cling to any surface. And finally, they go back to the ground, where they stand still like miniature statues, waiting for prey to come within a tongue's reach.

Sometimes, I see a male fence lizard (males have bulkier frame and head, and bold colors) popping up from behind one of the cacti. Unhurriedly, he crawls to reach the most protrusive peak of a foot-long volcanic lava rock. Then, as if he were in a gym, he starts doing push-ups. But it's not to stay in shape, even if some of my well-fed garden lizards could stand to lose a few milligrams. This up and down dance extends the abdomen and exposes the bright blue belly, which serves the dual function of attracting females while signaling other males, "Hey, dude, this is my territory!"

If a same-sex intruder shows up, things can escalate quickly into physical conflict, with biting and even some WWE-style wrestling, with both combatants standing on two feet in a full grip. Sometimes, blood is spilled.

Up close, I inspect the minute bodies of my western friends to double-check if these city dwellers have shorter, chubbier limbs than those living in the woods. So far, it looks like they do.

Once, in my yard, I was observing the legs of a male. He was carrying on his business less than an arm's length from me. Boldly. Fearlessly. Was this tiny reptile unafraid of me because of what I was wearing? I noted the color of my T-shirt and re-membered reading another paper by my super-prolific friend Dan on how the hues of our clothing can affect the escape behavior of this species. This shouldn't come as a shock con-sidering many animals see us as predators, and our demeanors can easily alter their reactions to our presence. Some bird species are attracted to colors that mirror their feathers, and vice-versa, are repelled by colors not present on themselves. This is known as the species-confidence hypothesis. Dan and colleagues tested this premise on western fence lizards, aware that males communicate with the blue patches on their throats and abdomens. Donning T-shirts of different hues in front of lizards, like models on a runway, they measured the individuals' reactions when approached, and how easy it was to noose them. It turned out that the westerns didn't bolt as much and were easier to capture when dark blue clothing was worn, showing a bias for this color. In a nutshell, what we wear can indirectly affect animals and modify their behavior. I keep this in mind when I dress in the morning and head out the door to observe nature.

And guess what color my T-shirt was when approaching the lizard in my yard up close and personal? Midnight blue.

• • •

One fine day on the bluffs, it was with great disbelief that I had an unexpected encounter: a real blast from the past. I was doing my customary walk with Genghis, when suddenly, sunbathing at the foot of a tree, there it was: an Italian wall lizard!

The story goes that these Italian reptiles arrived in 1994 at ground zero in San Pedro, the commercial port of Los Angeles, when someone brought a few of them back from a trip to Sicily. I swear, that *someone* wasn't me, even if I moved here around that time! Less than three decades were enough for a complete takeover by this tiny Italian invader.

Now, thousands of these settlers are crawling on walls in San Pedro and beyond. And these Italian lizards are not the only critters coming to sunny California in search of a new life;

hundreds of other invasive species are replacing the native fauna and flora. My favorite furry neighbor, the eastern squirrel, is another. But there is someone who wants to keep that from happening to the native lizards of South Cali. . . .

Dr. Greg Pauly is the curator of herpetology at the Natural History Museum of Los Angeles and the brain behind the Reptiles and Amphibians of Southern California project, aka RASCals, a group of observant citizen scientists, the "lizard hunters," who prowl the city and collect data for Dr. Pauly. Most of what we know about these colonizing wall lizards comes from community-gathered data rather than from biologists.

One can spot Greg, a sturdy man with a salt-and-pepper beard, baseball cap, Tevas, and backpack strolling on foot in the most remote corners of LA, armed with a twelve-foot lizard-catching pole as though he were hunting in the jungle. From my old days studying the home range and homing behavior of lizards in a natural reserve in Tuscany for my bachelor's thesis, I remember that noosing one of these reptiles is no piece of cake. Incredibly svelte, lizards can move like lightning when startled. Silence, slow movements, and patience are a must for gently working the thin loop around their neck. Once the noose is in place, it's easy to pull tight, and voilà, the lizard is caught, its tiny legs flailing and its body dangling from the pole as if it were on a swing.

. . .

The citizen lizard hunters are on the go, each on their own, contributing to our collective understanding. A middle-aged woman uses her iPhone to take pictures of an Indo-Pacific gecko scampering on her concrete-covered backyard; a young dad and his son in the upscale Hancock Park neighborhood unwearyingly seize a brown anole displaying its dewlap, a skin flap sagging from its throat. A seventy-year-old husband and wife team try to capture one of the alien *Podarcis* in a catch-and-release scenario, as though they were a couple of spry kids.

Pictures, notes, GPS positions, anything collected during these urban safaris ends up in the RASCals database. All this helps us learn more about these scaly vertebrates and sheds light on what is still unknown about our local cold-blooded biodiversity. In only a few years, Greg has put together a hefty troop of over eight thousand sharp-eyed naturalists. And the beauty of it is: Anyone can be a lizard hunter, the same way anyone can be a citizen scientist for one of the countless research projects ongoing around the world. Dolphins and whales in my ocean backyard included.

. . .

Genghis is exhausted. I can see that because his tongue almost touches the ground, leaving a trail of drool on the dirt path, and he completely misses the side-blotched lizard in plain sight on the edge of the trail. I tell him to sit, and I stop for a moment to watch this pocket-sized reptile.

Males of this species come in three varieties, each with a different throat hue: yellow, blue, and orange. Each color broadcasts to others what mating strategy an individual is going to use. This particular lizard on the bluffs is so orange throated he looks like he was dipped in carrot juice; this means he will defend his territory fiercely and mate with several females.

A rested Genghis finally spots the lizard, who scoots off, and my inspection is over.

We reach the LA Clippers billboard that marks the east end of the dirt trail and the start of asphalted civilization, then walk all the way back almost to the uppermost part of the cliff. A couple of red-tailed hawks soar over our heads in progressively smaller circles as if to wave goodbye, and then head back to their nest at the top of their old oak tree overlooking Playa Vista.

I stop to savor a breath of crisp air. At a distance, I see the ocean, and I miss it.

14

AMONG DOLPHINS

I dream of glassy waters; I dream of the rage of the open ocean. I dream of the dolphins and the whales. And I dream of being under the surface, among them, swimming and spinning freely, without the restraints of my land-bound human body. But this very night, I am not dreaming; I am wide-awake. My eyes have been open, staring at the dark ceiling since three o'clock in the morning.

I lie still, yet Genghis can tell I am not sleeping, and he bolts onto our bed, positioning himself next to me for his first morning rub. I wonder if he senses my excitement or if he is just nervous about the stack of Pelican cases by our front door, ready to go. He knows what Pelican cases are about.

Eyes shut, I let my thoughts wander to the last time I was out at sea.

It has been over a year, but it feels longer than that. I miss everything about being on the research boat: the salty air, the wind tingling my cheeks, the gentle, monotonous motion of the swells. I miss the large whales, the dolphins, the sea lions, the seabirds, the fish, and the sense of serenity and tranquility the pelagic waters bring. I miss how that uneasy, fidgety feeling of my hectic terrestrial life dissipates when the boat heads offshore and Los Angeles becomes a blurry line at the horizon. But I yearn mostly for the unknown, the unfathomed territory I might uncover when I am on the open ocean. And for so many years, that's what roused me from bed early in the morning to get set for heading seaward, to bundle up in layers and foul weather gear. There is so much to observe both at and beneath the surface, to discover and learn; and there is so much to protect. We call our planet Earth, yet most of our planet is ocean, and unexplored.

I feel now that the time I've spent in the company of marine animals as a field biologist was something I had begun to take for granted. How fortunate I've been to live this life on Earth, experiencing nature at its fullest, being wherever I craved to be, exploring, discovering, and attaining what I'd only dreamed of when I was just a little suburban girl. Curiosity, passion, and dedication brought me to where I am. Still, I think there was a good dose of luck too: to be born where and when I was, to be loved growing up, to have the freedom to see the natural world around me, to have found that bighearted, brilliant, and supportive soul who turned out to be my lifemate in this world.

Did I fail to fully appreciate my time sailing and diving in the Mediterranean and the Caribbean Seas, in the Gulf of Mexico, in the Atlantic and the Pacific? Seeing marine life every day, did I not value enough what I have been so privileged to observe far from shore, far from teeming cities and developed lands?

Away from the water for more than a year now, I muse about that intense sense of curiosity toward all ocean things I had when I was young. Has it been a tad diluted by passing time? By thousands of hours consumed by scanning the calm and rough ocean surface? By the endless clicks fired off with my cameras while perched on the railings of many boats? Have I gotten so used to dolphins and whales that I've lost some of that childhood pioneer inquisitiveness for the wilderness of the sea? I mull over these questions on this morning when I will once again resume my duties as a field marine biologist.

• • •

Like lettuce in a sandwich, I am wedged between Genghis, who is now back asleep with his back against my belly, and my better half, hugging me from the other side. I feel snug and loved between my two slices of warm bread.

There is still some time before the Grateful Dead ringtone of Charlie's alarm clock will blast its "Friend of the Devil" tune.

Genghis sprints off the bed gracelessly, stepping on my foot in the process. The smell of a skunk outside our bedroom awakened his senses, and he rockets toward the backyard window to inspect the intruder and fire off a few loud barks.

Charlie doesn't seem to notice, and I silently roll from under the covers so as not to wake him. I check the National Weather Service website for the Southern California marine forecast over a steaming cup of cappuccino. I want to be sure the ocean conditions haven't deteriorated overnight.

It reads: Monday – *Variable winds less than 5 kt becoming WSW 5 to 10 kt in the afternoon. Fog before 11 a.m. Mixed swell. . . . W 3 ft at 7 seconds and S 2 to 3 ft at 9 seconds. Wind waves 1-2 ft.*

Nooooooo! The weather has changed, for the worse. But there is no way I'll postpone the survey, not after so long away from the ocean.

It's worth a try, I think to myself. The fog usually lifts earlier than predicted, and on occasions, doesn't materialize at all.

I open the Pelican cases to ensure all the equipment is ready as Genghis runs my way with his usual puppy excitement. All this gear is undeniably more important than the skunk, and he plants himself in front of the door to ensure not being left behind.

"I lit out from Reno, I was trailed by twenty hounds, didn't get to sleep that night till the morning came around. . . ." reaches my ears from the end of the hallway. The alarm clock is singing, and it's almost time to go.

• • •

Shana and Kira wait with their duffle bags at the dock gate. They are about the same stature, with dark, long hair tied up in windproof ponytails. They both wear jeans, mandatory non-marking shoes, matching navy blue zip-front fleeces, and baseball caps with the Ocean Conservation Society logo.

As Charlie and I walk toward them along the seawall, I think about how long these ladies have been with us, rocked by the ups and downs of our nonprofit as well as the waves of the sea. Shana, the oldest of the two, has been part of our research crew since the late nineties; Kira, one of the most committed researchers I've ever worked with, has been with me for thirteen years now.

Volunteers requesting to become part of our team have

flooded my email inbox since I began my studies off California in 1996. However, once they face what is involved in becoming a field researcher out on the ocean, only the most intrepid make it through the six months of on-the-water and lab training required to become a skilled OCS researcher. Kira and Shana, perhaps with a few more lines and a little gray hair, and despite their professional careers ultimately moving them away from marine biology, still harbor the enthusiasm of their first days. As I approach my team and their smiles open up, I wish there were more like them protecting the untamed oceans.

The omnipresent virus imposes a no-hugs rule, but Genghis fills the awkward gap and launches toward Kira, licking wildly. As he pulls on the leash, my second cappuccino of the day spills from the stainless cup and onto my waterproof jacket. Of course, no one is fazed by our mutt's infamous gawkiness.

Shana and Kira are now staring at the new OCS boat as they might a wool sweater shrunken by a washing machine. With no funding on the horizon over the last year, Charlie and I had no choice but to sell our larger vessel and downsize to this pre-owned, cream-colored twenty-two-foot Shamrock, undeniably one of the smallest research powerboats we've ever had. Everyone here this morning, though, is acquainted with the accordion-like expanding and retracting of our nonprofit.

• • •

Embraced by a light haze, at the compulsory speed of five knots, we enter the Marina del Rey main channel. Then, as she has done hundreds of times before, Kira logs the first data entry of the day into the Toughbook laptop connected to a GPS that tracks the boat's position.

The familiar smell of guano fills our nostrils. Two dozen California sea lions nap on the hefty rocks of the breakwater just above the surface. A few sluggishly turn their heads as we pass, while the others remain piled on top of each other, uncaring. Perched above them, brown pelicans and western gulls stand abreast, all facing seaward like a battalion ready for conflict. Above all of them, a gargantuan American flag slow-dances back and forth to the beat of the light breeze.

As the boat leaves the aroma behind, Charlie parallels the shoreline heading south toward the lighthouse at Point Vicente in search of bottlenose dolphins. I walk to the bow of our boat to sit by myself and relish this moment to its fullest.

I inhale a breath of saline air, filling my lungs with it. Through binoculars, I scan the surface, searching for signs of marine life, any signs. I long for anything.

• • •

I felt that same emotion when I was hired as the principal investigator for one of the first marine mammal studies off the coast of Greece aboard the research sailboat *De Gomera* back in my early twenties. I remember too the insecurity I experienced back then: the doubts I had about my aptitude to accomplish the tasks that daily research at sea required, the fear of seasickness, and the dread of failing those who put their faith in me. But those adverse feelings were always overshadowed by my unwavering curiosity about all aquatic organisms coupled with the intense desire to be in that watery wilderness. I didn't let anything ruin my dreams of exploring the unknown lives of dolphins and whales. Failure wasn't an option.

Thousands of miles away and a few decades later, that eagerness is back. *I am* that passionate girl on the bowsprit of the *De Gomera*. Sitting on the boat above the secretive liquid world that extends as far as one can see off Los Angeles, my eyes and mind are wide open, ready to absorb whatever the ocean may offer.

• • •

The morning haze starts to lift and bursts of light pierce through the gray sheet that still conceals most of the sky. I turn around toward the stern to assure that everyone is okay.

Charlie steers the boat, silently, checking the radar and the bathymetry contours on the chart plotter. Kira and Shana scan the surface for marine mammals. They trade a few words, but mostly remain focused on their tasks, gazing oceanward, as I taught them.

Even Genghis, who buzzes around like a giant bee in his bright-yellow life jacket, is now on the lookout. His body extends in precarious equilibrium, back legs semi-anchored on a seat in the cockpit and front paws gripping the gunwale. His head swings side to side like a pendulum clock.

For a moment, through the zoom lens of my camera, I spy on Genghis's large, wet nose whiffing the air. It's his right nostril that does most of the work, and it makes sense since this nostril connects to the right-hand side of his brain, which is in charge of dealing with novel outside stimuli. Only when a smell becomes familiar does the left nostril tend to take over. I wonder what clues my dog's dazzling muzzle, infinitely more sensitive than mine, is picking up right now. Even here, away from the trees and grass of the bluffs, there have to be a multitude of novel scents to absorb from the nearby milieu.

As we pass a line of wet-suited surfers waiting for a new set of swells near Manhattan Beach pier, I go back to watching the water.

"Bottlenose, three o'clock, five hundred meters!" I yell as I spot a couple of dark dorsal fins slicing the surface.

That's enough to put the entire team into full motion.

And there is no need for words: everyone already knows what to do. Charlie speeds up. He points our small open boat into the oncoming wavelets in the direction of the animals, keeping an eye on my arm that points him toward the dolphins.

"Six bottlenose, two o'clock, three hundred meters." I fine-tune my first assertion, now that I have a gross count of the dorsal fins surfacing every twenty seconds or so.

Kira brings the stopwatch and camera on deck and readies herself to tally the individuals in the group and observe their behavior. Next to her, Shana dutifully keys in the first log-form entry for this sighting, noting weather and ocean conditions, species, first character spotted, distance, and range. Charlie slowly parallels the dolphin group, careful to keep the sun behind us so the photos will be well-lit. My dog's body is tense; his head is now like one of those bobblehead figurines, moving up and down and side to side, almost as though he's counting the individuals in the pod. I adjust my Canon around the neck, set to take pictures.

A couple of adult dolphins slide along our hull to ride the boat's bow wave. Hanging slightly off the railing, my face is now within spitting distance from their smooth, large heads. I watch as their fluid bodies dance and whirl below the surface. Then, in synchrony, they turn sideways and glance at me. Our eyes meet, and for a moment, that invisible line between our two worlds disappears. A shiver runs down my spine and the hairs on my arms stand up like fans at a Rolling Stones concert. Maybe due to the chilly wind but probably just for the thrill of being here. Once again, *among* dolphins.

I have followed flukeprints for more than twenty-five years off California and observed, up close and personal, this metropolitan bottlenose population that journeys back and forth along the coast. I have written several scientific papers and books about them. I now better understand their occurrence, frequency, and distribution in these ocean neighborhoods, what they eat, and where their favorite feeding spots are. I have learned about their traveling, socializing, diving, and mating activities, and I have met some of the other species they hang out with. I can often tell when a female delivers a new calf, whether an individual has developed more skin lesions in the last year, and the average size of their fluid social groups. With my team, we have compared tens of thousands of dorsal fin photographs to individually identify them.

Despite all of it, I have only scratched the surface of their covert existence. I know close to nothing of their experiences or how they live their lives. What goes on under the layer separating my reality from that of a dolphin is, for the most part, still a mystery. They are animals dear to me, and at the same time, they are aliens existing in a realm I cannot access. When, and only when, *they* decide to share moments with me, can I observe their antics and learn. And not only about them, but from them as well.

The wild, free-ranging dolphins and whales have taught me about the intrinsic beauty of simplicity. They have shown me how to live a life that doesn't need to consume and destroy everything around it to thrive.

Cetaceans, oceans, and nature as a whole have the power to lessen our unending need for material things. They can change us and make us better humans by prompting our species to see the grandeur around us and reconnect to our wild side. I've seen it happen to my volunteers, and to me, in the Caribbean Sea, on the shores of the unspoiled reserves of the Yucatán Peninsula, and here, just seaward of the Los Angeles metropolis. Listening to the intricate songs of humpback whales, eavesdropping on the matriarchal societies of orcas, watching bottlenose dolphins cleverly cooperate in catching prey, have transformed me. Dolphins remind me of my connection to the great tree of life, and that living in harmony with other species is essential to our planet's survival. Through observing blues, grays, fins, seis, humpbacks, sperms, and other goliaths of the sea, I've witnessed how strength and power can go hand in hand with grace and kindness.

Wilderness, on land and out on the ocean, always has

something to impart if we can allow ourselves to look around and listen.

• • •

When the virus slowed international shipping and kept cruise ships, local ferries, and tourist boats tied to their docks, it increased the stress level for many of us humans. But our seas grew more silent, which likely eased life for marine mammals as the anthropogenic volume of our world turned down. Of course, this was only a temporary reprieve for them. It does, though, provide a glimpse into how their existence once was, and what it could be again if there was a global human commitment to reduce ocean noise.

With humankind in hiding, not only cetaceans breathed easier in a new liberty. Voices of rebounding nature began to echo everywhere around the planet. Quickly. Elephant seals took over a popular beach at Point Reyes in California. A puma descended from the Andes to explore the previously hectic capital of Santiago de Chile. Baby rabbits hopped unhindered along the roads of Christchurch, New Zealand. Wild boars conquered an eight-lane thoroughfare in Barcelona, Spain. In search of food, a flock of geese waddled their way into a temple in Nagaon, India, and macaques foraged near the deserted stands of the Johari Bazar in Jaipur. Mountain goats strolled along the streets of Llandudno in Wales, while cows roamed unrestricted on a once-tourist-packed Corsican beach. Sika deer grazed near a sushi restaurant in urban Nara, Japan. Peacocks went shopping in the Middle Eastern city of Dubai. Ducks wandered the previously traffic-jammed streets of Paris while a wild fox meandered through the heart of London.

With *Homo sapiens* in lockdown, the novel coronavirus revealed what a world with less human impact might be like. How hastily other organisms can bounce back when we take ourselves out of the equation, even if only for a brief moment; when we stop imposing our power over other nonhuman beings. As Mother Nature has proved to our species during the pandemic, we can still reverse many of our harmful impacts and spare the oceans from destruction. We still have a window of opportunity to halt the damage. We still have ten percent of large fish; some blue whales, a few vaquitas and right whales out there; some coral reefs are still alive. A virus taught us how to slow down and reminded us that we are not the masters of the universe: we must hold onto that knowledge in order to set a true course forward.

• • •

Heightened by a rekindling of inquisitiveness thanks to the nature I discovered swarming around me while on terrestrial lockdown, I feel reawakened and rebooted. As someone who has always preferred the freedom and silence of the open ocean to the roar of a metropolis, being stranded at home and undertaking an urban safari in my backyard and neighborhood helped me appreciate where I live in and its wildlife, and perhaps has improved my field research at sea as well. Everything in nature is interwoven, and observing more "ordinary" species up close in my garden allowed me to better grasp that natural fabric of life. When we look at the creatures around us through the lens of animal behavior, we understand and respect that they have their own purposes on Earth, which have just as much value as ours.

My work as a field cetologist and environmentalist requires the right state of mind coupled with an overdose of enthusiasm. While stuck at home, I faced despair and loneliness at a level I had never experienced before. But the wildlife swarming nearby lifted the bleakness and unearthed a sense of hopefulness. I came to see the value of bonding with nature for my own emotional well-being. I found internal peace when I attuned to being still. And I felt an even more profound love for all animals, from AT the paper wasp to the stealthy coyotes. This period of uncertainty helped me better understand that the distinctions between species are more questions of holistic degree than rigid definition.

My slow, steady explorations of the wild nearby also made my power of observation more acute, as I learned to notice what I'd ignored before at my very own home. And now, back on the ocean among dolphins, I hope to build on what the surrounding biota taught me during this past year. I hope to hold on to that revived inquisitiveness, to that gentler rhythm that allows me to breathe and to see the grandness all around me.

As I resurface after the unexpected, tempestuous time of confinement and change, I feel an obligation toward nature, near and far, that has so enriched my life. And I feel reinforced in my belief in the urgent need to protect Mother Earth.

• • •

We humans are pieces of a glorious and magnificent web of life where all is connected and interdependent. Each species, marine or otherwise, has a part to play that is sometimes evident, sometimes not. Living things have a function beyond themselves in that they fit into the fabric of biodiversity by feeding on or supporting other life forms.

These natural connections and linkages, at sea or on land, are often hard to visualize.

By looking outside ourselves, perhaps even abandoning the comfort of our human perspective of the world, we can discover things that have and will change our existence and can create a stronger bond with all forms of life. Strengthening this bond is essential to grasping why sustainability is so important in today's world, where resources we once thought to be infinite are dwindling.

As science and technology progress at unprecedented rates, we grow closer than ever to knowing how nature works, but we still have a long way to go toward understanding where our place is in the natural cycle of things. This is because many human cultures and religious doctrines encourage the belief that we are masters of our world. The earth, too many of us are taught, is ours to subdue and establish dominion over.

We look at expanses of wilderness and see timber to be harvested or undeveloped agricultural assets. We see our oceans both as infinite trash dumps and endless sources of human-kind's sustenance. We rarely take the time to fathom the intrinsic value of nature to our own well-being or the well-being of the nonhuman biodiversity it supports. We have an excuse, or at least we *had* one in the past when we didn't know that unbridled development was adversely impacting Earth. But that excuse is now gone, and we need to wake up from the unsustainable dream we are dreaming. A purely economic and market-driven view of the world will not lead us to a happy future. Being the oceans' superpredators won't lead us anywhere.

Perhaps human salvation lies in our connection to

nature, nearby and distant. The choice now before us is how will we shape our planet given our unique abilities as a highly capable and particularly brainy species.

People talk about reconnecting to nature as though we could ever disconnect from it. We cannot. We are natural creatures of a natural world. The connection is not simply a spiritual one, although many of us feel something greater than ourselves when we gaze at the stars above our heads or stand at the seashore feeling the ground tremble from the crashing waves. The connection I am speaking of is physical. The environment on land and sea shapes us, and we depend on our respective biota. This connection is the fleeting balance of nature upon which our very existence depends. Understanding more about how this delicate balance is maintained can help us make it more resilient. And resilience, in evolutionary and biological terms, is a very good attribute for survival.

"Only if we understand can we care.
Only if we care will we help.
Only if we help shall they be saved."

—JANE GOODALL

Is there a moral to these stories? I suppose that is something personal to each of us. I know that I learned things from living through the pandemic, things I think will help me be a better scientist and perhaps a better, more observant and empathetic person. Uncertain times being what they are, I hope my experiences may coalesce with those of readers and bring a little solace when things go south. In that spirit, I respectfully submit the following:

IDEAS FOR UNCERTAIN TIMES

1. Open your eyes and heart to the wilderness around you with curiosity; you'll discover something new every day.

2. Hold tight to joyful memories; they can rescue you when you need them.

3. Relax and meditate, in whatever ways work for you.

4. Find beauty in *all* creatures.

5. Respect and empathize with other beings sharing the Earth with us. We are not the only emotional species on this planet. Act accordingly.

6. Learn from animals (and plants); they have a lot to teach us.

7. Give voice to the voiceless.

8. Each of us has a say in the future of our planet. Speak up!

9. Don't wait for things to change; change them and inspire others to do the same.

10. Embrace our connection to nature, as human salvation lies therein.

ACKNOWLEDGMENTS

I am deeply indebted to Carl Safina, a terrific person and marvelous author. His kindhearted words of encouragement, suggestions, and moral support have been pivotal not only for the making of this book but also for me as an author.

I am grateful to my friends, colleagues, and animal devotees: Dan Blumstein, Craig Stanford, and Marc Bekoff for reviewing the first draft of this manuscript, as well as Andy Rotherham and Marcy Saylan for their comments. *Grazie mille* to my brother Gio for his always valuable insights, and to my parents for leading me toward nature at an early age.

I am especially obliged to my editor at Heyday, Marthine Satris. Her guidance, enthusiasm, thoughtful critiques, and firm belief that my stories need to be read have been invaluable. Thank you, as well, to Emmerich Anklam, Diane Lee, Molly Woodward, and everyone else on the Heyday team. It has been a true delight working with you all!

This book would not exist without Charlie, love of my life, husband, best friend, and personal editor extraordinaire: Thanks for believing in me, supporting me all the way, challenging me to be a better writer, and for just being you.

ABOUT THE AUTHOR

Maddalena Bearzi is president and cofounder of Ocean Conservation Society. She holds a Ph.D. in biology and a postdoctorate from UCLA, and she has been involved in studying marine mammals and other species, with a conservation bias, since 1990. Her research on dolphins and whales off California represents one of the longest investigations worldwide. She has published several scientific peer-reviewed papers, and she is coauthor of *Beautiful Minds: The Parallel Lives of Great Apes and Dolphins* (Harvard University Press) and author of *Dolphin Confidential: Confessions of a Field Biologist* (University of Chicago Press). Her work and books have been covered by CNN, NPR, KPCC, *Al Jazeera America*, the Hallmark Channel, the *Los Angeles Times*, the *Wall Street Journal*, the *Huffington Post*, and *American Scientist*, among others. Bearzi has also been a writer for numerous media, including *National Geographic*. Born and raised in Italy, she now lives in Los Angeles with her husband and dog.